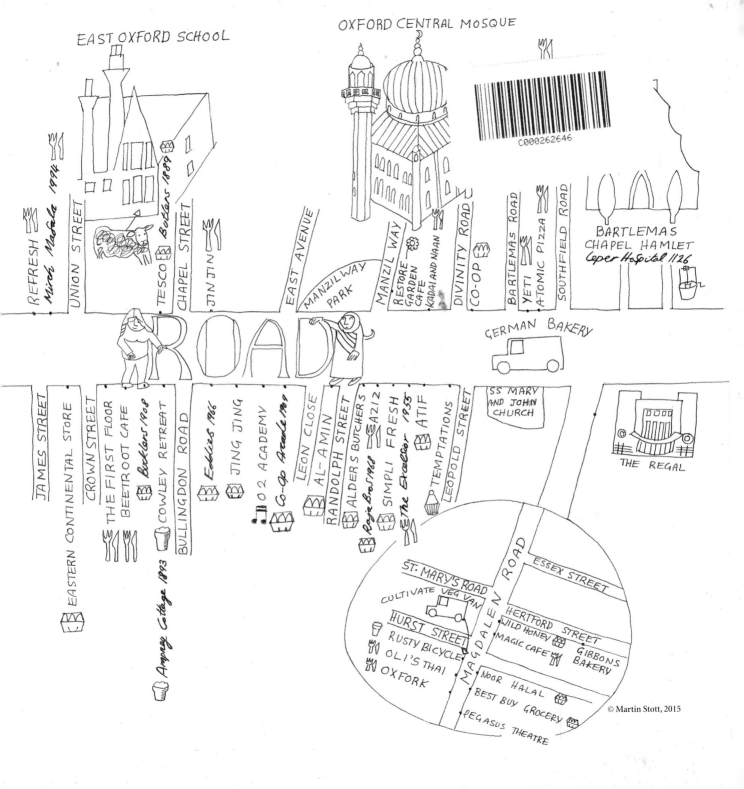

© Martin Stott, 2015

To my daughters Nadine and Alice who shared the joys of exploring
our neighbourhood and the pleasures of cooking.

THE
COWLEY
ROAD
COOKBOOK

Culinary tales and recipes from Oxford's most eclectic street

MARTIN STOTT

AN OXFORDFOLIO PUBLICATION FOR SIGNAL BOOKS

Signal

An Oxfordfolio publication [www.oxfordfolio.co.uk] for

Signal Books
www.signalbooks.co.uk

Signal Books Limited
36 Minster Road
Oxford OX4 1LY

Designed by Nick Withers
Project editor James Harrison
Cover and food illustrations by Michael Gabriel © 2015
Street illustration (endpapers) by Alex Singleton
Maps by Sebastian Ballard © 2015

ISBN: 978-1-909930-32-2
Printed and bound in England by Henry Ling Ltd, The Dorset Press, Dorchester

Contents

Introduction

Cowley Road is a place, but also a state of mind. On a map of Oxford it appears simply as the B480. A visitor approaching the city along it from the south east will pass by the BMW car plant, an unfamiliar sight to many whose image of Oxford is more 'dreaming spires' than screaming tyres. The ever-popular 'Inspector Morse' TV series used Cowley Road as a backdrop or major location for many episodes; a useful contrast to the cloistered colleges of the city.

Cowley Road is a complex combination of physical form and the imprint left by various overlapping and intermingling waves of migration: pilgrims, traders, scholars, refugees, immigrants, residents and visitors upon a street that has become over time, one of the most vibrant, eclectic and ethnically diverse in England. This book both charts and celebrates this unique street's story.

It is both a culinary book and a social and cultural history of the street and surrounding area stretching over almost 900 years. As such it is about food and its place in the lives of local people through the ages. In exploring that history it also becomes a celebration of solidarity, mutuality, hospitality, neighbourliness, social and racial integration and sheer hard work.

Cowley Road has developed a distinctive food history and culture and there is much to be proud of. However, it is not some Mediterranean island, French province or Italian region, with their distinctive foods and recipes honed over centuries to reflect the best of local produce. But the 'terroir' that those localities celebrate, that 'sense of place', embodied in certain characteristic qualities, has its urban equivalent in the food culture of Cowley Road; distinctive, constantly changing, often memorable, with a desire to experiment, it is a reflection of the locality and its exuberance.

Cowley Road has evolved gradually into a place to find interesting food over at least the past 70 years. But it is not a sophisticated 'foodie heaven'. How could it be when the street is lined with pubs, bars and takeaways, primarily aimed at a student/low income clientele? Its attraction is its chaotic nature, its constant change and its diversity. In this context, food outlets – cafés, takeaways, shops, restaurants, wholesalers and all kinds of low cost pop-up opportunities including vans

An area that is well-supplied with charity shops, car washes …

selling everything from fruit and veg to specialist cakes and breads, can thrive – quirky, cheap-jack, exotic, innovative and occasionally heavenly. But they jostle for space in an area that is also well-supplied with pubs, bike shops, barbers, 'head shops', tattoo parlours, sex shops, bookies, pawn brokers, charity shops, car washes and the other essentials of daily life.

But they benefit too from being cheek by jowl with the practically unique. Where else would you find a robe-maker, customers ranging from Bishops to Vice-Chancellors, next to a fried chicken takeaway?

Cowley Road has its darker side too, with boarded up premises and a few, usually temporary, outlets with rather indeterminate purposes, which are often no more than fronts for drug dealing, money laundering, prostitution or worse, as the national publicity around the 'Operation Bullfinch' convictions in 2013 and the follow up Serious Case Review in 2015, demonstrated.

There are a lot of interesting meals to be had on and around Cowley Road in a range of cafés, restaurants, takeaways, gastropubs, coffee shops and the recent phenomenon of dessert parlours, that would be the envy of any other city in England. But this is not a restaurant guide. Plenty of other people do that already and do it well. However food shops are too often seen as 'part of the furniture' and are overlooked.

Instead this book reflects the locality and my experiences of living on and around Cowley Road for over 35 years as a participant in the processes of its evolution, variously as parent, shopper, enthusiastic grower, cook, local councillor, campaigner and community activist.

In interviewing people involved in shops, restaurants, cafés and allotment growing in east Oxford, I have been struck by a couple of shared perspectives. One is pride in what has been created. Everyone recognises that the chaotic exuberance of Cowley Road contributes enormously to Oxford as a whole and to an atmosphere that benefits everybody: shoppers, visitors and entrepreneurs alike. The other is a concern that a tipping point has been reached and that this diversity is genuinely under threat. Even ten years

Children getting a hot meal during World War Two (below) in the Municipal Restaurant in St. Clements.

ago the idea that Cowley Road might go the way of any other English city street and become another 'clone town' product was seen as laughable; wrong demographic (too poor), wrong land holdings (properties too small to be worth the trouble), wrong part of town. At the start of the century there was one big chain supermarket on the street, Tesco, which has been a fixture on Cowley Road since 1962. Now there are three of the big multiples, and well over a dozen chain coffee shops, restaurants and takeaways. While writing this book one of the mainstays of Cowley Road since the 1950s, 'The Excelsior' café closed as a direct result of these trends. Out of this come several themes that run through the book.

Oxford's Cowley Road is nothing if not a celebration of multiculturalism through a sharing of food culture, when the very idea of integration and the mutual respect and celebration of difference seem to be under attack. The mutuality and diversity of feasting and celebration such as the annual Cowley Road Carnival is a regular, noisy, exuberant and joyful re-statement of what Cowley Road is all about. Eid, Diwali, Christmas and Hanukkah are all marked in ways that people can participate in and enjoy.

Cowley Road is also all about hospitality and mutuality, both in times of hardship and of plenty – from the lepers and pilgrims of 13th-century Bartlemas through to the still continuing presence of religious and monastic orders in the locality, via the Municipal Restaurant on St Clements during the rationing of the Second World War and after. It only closed in 1974. That tradition has continued in cafés like the Excelsior and more recently, Refresh.

Another important theme is that of self-reliance and sharing in the produce and skills to be found on community gardens and allotments – from 'Dig for Victory' to the present day. Sharing food, at least partly outside the money economy through initiatives like community kitchen project 'DinnerTime', and 'Abundance' who collect and distribute surplus fruit from orchards, back gardens and roadside trees, has strong links in the neighbourhood.

I explore all of these themes in this book and in doing so hope to make a small contribution to Cowley Road's rich history.

The noisy, exuberant and joyful Cowley Road Carnival.

ABOUT THE RECIPES

The recipes in this book, apart from some of the earlier, historical ones, are drawn from ingredients readily obtainable from shops on or around Cowley Road. An exception to this is fish. There is good fish to be found on Cowley Road but it is mostly dried or frozen. This is perhaps a reflection of the 'localness' of the food on the street. After all Oxford is about as far away as you can get from the sea in England. The recipes have also come out of cooking for a family, learning as I go along, making mistakes, using the materials at hand and trying not to be too extravagant. Both learning how to shop on Cowley Road and growing my own food has been crucial to that. Allotments, orchards and community gardens in east Oxford also provide a surprisingly large amount of the food to be found locally, including a substantial quantity in some of the restaurants.

As the book is at least in part a social and cultural history of Cowley Road through food, about a quarter of the recipes are historical in some sense or other. These are dotted around the earlier chapters at least roughly reflecting their social and historical context. Some of them are for meals that we wouldn't eat much now, like pottage, but they were popular at the time with people who lived locally then and are worth a try now. To make them more readily useable as recipes I have updated them where I can, while retaining their original spirit. Chapter 5 is dedicated to contemporary recipes and the selection is based on local and personal choices.

As with many people, I like reading cookbooks, have collected favourite recipes over the years and have experimented as I have successfully grown something new or something has taken my fancy in one of the many fascinating shops. My inspiration has come in significant degree from cooks who I consider to be from the saner and more down-to-earth end of cookery writing, like Felicity Cloake, Sam and Sam Clark, Rose Elliot, Hugh Fearnley-Whittingstall, Claudia Roden, Jack Monroe, Rose Gray, Ruth Rodgers, Antonio Carluccio and Yotam Ottolenghi, along with intrepid foragers Richard Mabey and John Lewis Stempel. I acknowledge a debt to them all.

CHAPTER ONE

Cufa's Leah to Cowley Road

The place name Cowley comes from Cufa's leah, 'cufah' meaning a clearing in woodland for agricultural or pastoral purposes and 'ley' being a clear tract between woodland and river. The Romans kept away from the marshy banks of the Thames, preferring to establish settlements on the higher ground of overlooking hills. The first reference to Oxford as a place is in 911AD when it was part of a system of fortified burgs to defend Wessex. By about 1290 the little village of what was to become Cowley was called Cohfleye, but the east Oxford area was largely agricultural until the late 18th century. The only significant habitation east of the river before the developments in St Clements parish in the late 16th century was the leper hospital known as St Bartholomew's Hospital. However Cowley Road, though not named as that until the 19th century, existed as part of the drove road (an ancient roadway along which cattle and sheep were taken to market) from Oxford to London over the top of Shotover Hill from earliest times.

ST BARTHOLOMEW'S LEPER HOSPITAL: A TRADITION OF SANCTUARY AND HOSPITALITY

One mile from the Eastgate in the medieval city walls and over the petty pont [now Magdalen] bridge (where beggars could fruitfully beg) was St Bartholomew's Hospital, set back from the drove road between Oxford and London and known by 1605 as St Bartholomew's Way. The hospital building itself is the only former leper hospital in England that is still inhabited. The site of the hamlet, now called Bartlemas, just off Cowley Road still exists, set back from the current road and hidden behind high hedges. Established in 1126 by Henry I as a leper hospital for the city and endowed with £23 5d, it held twelve lepers and a chaplain. After 1321 lepers were no longer admitted and the hospital and chapel were transferred to Oriel College in 1329 by Edward III. Eight aged and infirm 'almsmen' were installed, providing that two of them were 'hale' [healthy] and could carry out farming duties on the fifteen acres of fields and a grove of fruit trees. Each was allocated a garden for their own cultivation.

Bartlemas was a major pilgrimage destination in the 14th century with a holy well in the grounds of the chapel.

❦ POTTAGE

A very common dish would have been 'pottage' essentially a form of broth or soup, something cooked in a pot and fairly liquid so that the contents at the bottom didn't burn. The most common type of pottage would have been made of vegetables that were easily grown and known as 'green porray'. Barley, rye or wheat would have made up the basis of a of a 'frumenty' pottage at Bartlemas. Meat, if available, would have been added by wealthier people and such luxuries as sugar, saffron, almonds and eggs would have also made an appearance on their tables. These versions of pottage were called 'morrews'. Pottage is of course the origin of modern day soup.

This is a recipe using ingredients that a Bartlemas almsman in the 13th century would have been familiar with. The vegetables and herbs used would have been those available during that season, so the recipe is flexible. Serves four.

1 fresh cabbage
2 medium onions
2 leeks, whole
2–3 medium carrots
Handful of peas (fresh or dried)
Handful of barley
1¼ pints stock ('broth') chicken, beef or vegetable
A selection of herbs including sage, parsley, mint or dill

Soak the barley for 15 minutes. Wash and chop the vegetables. Pod the peas. Thinly slice the onions. Make up the stock using boiling water. Put all the ingredients together in a large pan. Bring to the boil and simmer for 20 minutes.

Serve with chunks of wholemeal bread and mead if available.

❦ MEDIEVAL APPLE TART

This is a recipe which only the top strata of society could have eaten because of the expense of spices, which became more common from the 12th century – but the chaplain at Bartlemas would probably have eaten such a pie as the hospital was well supplied with fruit trees. Referred to as 'tartys in apples' the recipe dates from 1381.
Serves 4–6.

4 apples
4 pears
2 tbsp flour
2 oz chopped dried figs
2 oz raisins
6 oz sugar
1 tsp cinnamon
½ tsp nutmeg
½ tsp ginger
½ tsp saffron
1 tbsp lemon juice
A little red wine or rum
½ pint water
1½ lbs shortcrust pastry

Peel and core the apples and pears and slice them thinly. Put the cores and skins in a saucepan with the water and a little sugar, leave to boil until reduced by one third. Make the pastry (if you want pastry).

Toss the fresh fruit in a bowl with the flour, then add the sugar and the dried fruits with the spices, lemon juice and wine or rum. Allow to steep a little.

Roll out the pastry and line a nine inch pie dish, reserving enough for the lid.

Fill the pie with the mixed fruit and strain over the juice from the cores and skins.

Cover with the pastry lid and bake at 180°c/gas mark 4 for 30 minutes.

The chapel at Bartlemas in the 1890s.

It was importantly a place of refuge, offering sanctuary to the sick and a place of hospitality for pilgrims who were an important source of income. Bartlemas established a tradition of hospitality for the visitor and the vulnerable alike, which has continued in east Oxford through the centuries to the present day.

In the 14th century the almsmen would have cultivated a familiar, but to us limited, range of vegetables including leeks, cabbages, beans, peas, carrots, turnips, parsnips and onions. Potatoes didn't arrive in Britain until 1586 (thanks to Virginian colonists) and it was another 200 years before they were a common crop. Herbs such as garlic, parsley, sage, mint, dill, thyme and spring onions were important for flavour and medicinal purposes. Apart from these, the diet of ordinary country people consisted of 'black' bread, milk, cheese, eggs and occasional bacon or fowl.

Medieval almsmen would have kept hens and ducks too, but fish, except for occasional pieces of dried cod, known as stockfish because the cook would beat the dried cod with a club or stock before cooking, would have been off their menu. Eggs and game would be a significant part of this medieval menu. Foraging for everything from nuts and blackberries to mushrooms would have been popular as would trapping wood pigeons, hare, rabbit and other game. Fruit trees, particularly apples or 'permains' as they were known, were common. There were about 1,500 early varieties of apple, and cider making was common, as was ale, which was widely used in cooking. Other fruit such as pears, cherries, plums, grapes, damsons and walnuts were also cultivated. The land at Bartlemas, was considered very fruitful and the hamlet is still surrounded by allotments, one of which I have cultivated since 1988.

Medieval farming on the King's lands and those of powerful landowners such as the Oxford colleges hadn't changed much since Roman times. Wheat, barley oats, rye, vetches and beans were all grown in the fields which before enclosure were divided into strips.

OXFORD IN THE ENGLISH CIVIL WAR

Oxford became Charles I's capital in the early part of the Civil War (1642-51) and Bartlemas played a significant part in its siege. A nearby grove of some 500 elm trees was cut down in 1643 by Royalist forces to prevent it giving cover to Parliamentary troops. They nevertheless occupied the Hospital with its convenient water supply from adjacent springs, and stabled their horses in the Chapel, stripping the lead from its roof to make bullets, and stopping up the holy well on the grounds of 'papist superstition'.

The area was known for its good grazing, and on 3 June, 1646, 100 horsemen came out of the Eastgate in an attempt to drive *'cattle which were grazing near Cowley'* into the City to feed the besieged residents. The attempt was foiled with the loss of three lives, before Cromwellian troops went on to take the City later that month. They were probably fortified by something called a 'Great Oxford-shire Cake'. *The Compleat Cook* of 1658 has the recipe which is clearly intended to feed a goodly multitude such as a detachment of soldiers. There is no modern version.

St Bartholomew's Hospital was almost completely destroyed in the Civil War but was rebuilt in 1649, the same year as the second Oxford mutiny led by Leveller factions in the Cromwellian army, which resulted in the execution in the city of two ringleaders, Privates Biggs and Piggen on 18 September that year. The radical Oxford horticulturalist Ralph Austen who was involved in the purge of Royalists from the University following the siege of 1646 and almost

❈ GREAT OXFORD-SHIRE CAKE

"Take a peck of flower by weight, and dry it a little, & a pound and a halfe of Sugar one ounce of Cinamon, half an ounce of Nutmegs, a quarter of an ounce of Mace and Cloves, a good spoonfull of Salt, beat your Salt and Spice very fine, and searce it, and mix it with your flower and Sugar; then take three pound of butter and work in the flower, it will take three hours working; then take a quart of Ale-yeast, two quarts of Cream half a pint of Sack, six grains of Amber-greece dissolved in it halfe a pint of Rosewater, sixteen Eggs, eight of the Whites, mix these wit the flower, and knead them well together, then let it lie warm by your fire till your Oven be hot, which must be a little hotter than for manchet; when you make it ready for your Oven, put to your Cake six pound of currans, two pound of raisins, of the Sun stoned and minced, so make up your Cake, and set it in your oven stopped close; it will take three hours a baking; when baked, take it out and frost it over with the white of an Egge and Rosewater, well beat together and strew fine Sugar upon it and then set it again into the Oven that it may Ice."

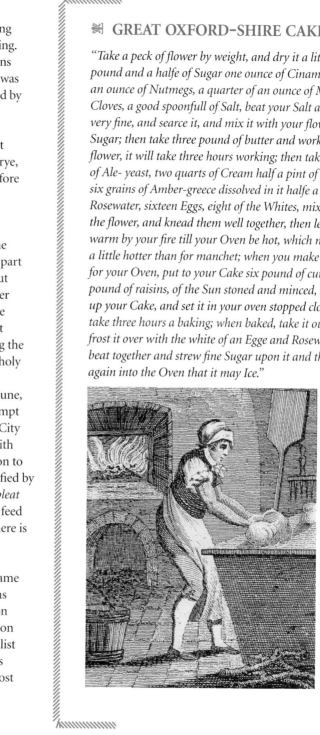

certainly fought here, was an advocate of the mass planting of fruit trees writing in his *Treatise of Fruit Trees* that '*I know from what I now doe yearly that my selfe with two workmen to help me might prepare Twenty thousand Plants yearly at least;*'. He argued that mankind had been cut off from the good apples of Eden at the Fall and that a good Christian must regain paradise by planting the best trees. He produced many varieties of fruit tree.

Leprosy had largely died out in England by the 16th century and the hospital evolved into almshouses and as a refuge from the Plague and other diseases, providing Oriel College scholars with a refuge 'in times of pestilential sickness' which occasionally swept the city. For example as recently as the 1832 cholera outbreak, patients were sent there for convalescence. However by 1864 the number of almsmen had dwindled to four and they were transferred to the newly opened Workhouse on Cowley Road.

The chaplain's house became Bartlemas Farmhouse and the area was farmed by the Pether family until the early 20th century with the chapel being used as a cattle byre until 1913. The land owned by Oriel College was parcelled up in 1927, becoming playing fields for their students, a bowling green and allotments.

OF BEES AND BOTANICAL GARDENS

In 1676 Robert Plot who went on to become Keeper of the Ashmolean Museum published *The Natural History of Oxfordshire*. Amongst the other creatures surveyed, the fish in the Thames caught his eye.

'*. . we have a sort in the River Isis that we call here a pride, of the long cartilaginous smooth kind. . . Beside the pride. . . we have another sort of fish plentiful in the Cherwell (scarce ever found in Isis, but below the place where the rivers join). . . and that is a fish that they call a finscale, somewhat like a roach. . .*' as well as chub, perch, tench and the occasional salmon.

'*How these salmon should come up so high has been much wondered at by some since so many mills and locks stand in the way. . .*'.

He goes on to speculate that this is not so improbable as most of the mills and locks have back streams to carry off water when it is too plentiful '*. . over which the leap is but very inconsiderable*'.

Plot was also interested in bees. Being a University man he retells a story of the arrival of Cardinal Wolsey, Henry VIII's Chancellor, in Oxford in 1520 to be the Professor of Publick Rhetorick. Wolsey was elected to Corpus Christi College, one of the major landowners in east Oxford, which was known by its founder as the College of Bees. Appropriately, Wolsey

'*. . . was welcomed thither by a swarm of bees, which to signify the incomparable sweetness of his eloquence, settled themselves over his head under the leads of his study (at the west end of the cloister) where they continued about 130 years.*'

In 1630 a roof renovation disturbed the bees,

'*. . . their stall was taken and with it an incredible mass of honey: but the bees as presaging their intended and imminent destruction (whereby they were never known to have swarmed before) did that Spring (to preserve that their famous kind) send down a fair swarm into the President's garden, which in the year 1633 yielded two swarms one whereof pitched in the garden for the President; the other they sent up as a new colony to preserve the memory of this mellifluous Doctor. . . .*'

Plot was writing during the reign of Charles II, so naturally they were Royalist bees and so according to him, when the city and the college was taken over by Parliamentarians in 1648, rather than give honey to the occupying forces '*. . . they instantly declined, and came shortly to nothing*'.

Not long before, in 1621, the Physic Garden now the Botanical Gardens, beside Magdalen Bridge was established in Oxford. It was the first in the country. The £5,000 (£3.5m in today's money) donated to endow it was all spent on its grandiose construction, leaving nothing to pay its first Superintendent Jacob Bobart, who when appointed in 1642, had to make ends meet by selling fruit grown in the garden.

Just up the road a Jewish man called Jacob, opened the first coffee shop in England in 1652 on the site of what is now the Grand Café on the High Street. Cromwell had just legalised the conduct of lawful business by Jews in England and it was the first business to be opened by a Jew in Oxford since medieval times.

Across the river, St Clement's, at the bottom of the road to London, (the causeway over the river was known as Londonwyke Street) began to grow in the late 1500s as:

'tradesmen were increasingly attracted to a parish near enough to the city to supply the Oxford market, yet remote enough to enable them to escape the restrictions and expenses imposed upon city artisans and shopkeepers'.

Consequently the area became the residence for a significant number of traders who supplied produce for consumption in the City and University. One such trader was Ben Tyrrell who in the 1740s was doing a roaring trade in his mutton pies from an outlet on the High Street. He advertised in verse:

All ye that love what's nice and rarish,
At Oxford in St Mary's parish,
Ben Tyrrell, cook of high Renown,
To please the palates of the Gown
At three-pence each makes Mutton-Pies
Which thus he begs to advertise.

O bear me witness Isis' sons!
Pierce but the crust- the gravy runs;
The taster licks his lips and cries,
'O Rare Ben Tyrrell's Mutton Pies.'

There was a wide range of stalls such as his, and street markets in the city thrived until the latter part of the 18th century, when they were moved and consolidated into one large indoor market in 1774 – the still surviving Covered Market. This independence of spirit by the residents, led to St Clement's parish, despite its proximity to the city, maintaining its own identity and only being incorporated into the City in 1836. This was a reflection of the growth of the city eastwards, as the parish population grew from just 413 in 1801 to 1,836 by 1831.

ENCLOSURE COMES TO OXFORD

By the 18th century land ownership in east Oxford was largely in the hands of a few colleges: Christ Church, Brasenose, Oriel and Corpus Christi. The other key landowners were Donnington Hospital, which owned land passed to it from

✠ POACHED RIVER FISH WITH FRUIT

This is the kind of dish that someone getting fish from the Thames would have cooked at this time. The recipe dates from 1660. Serves 3–4.

1 lb river fish e.g. perch, pike bream or tench, filleted
4 oz sliced onion • 2 oz currants • 2 oz dates, chopped
2oz prunes, chopped • 1 oz red currrants
1 tbsp cornflour • 1 pint water • 2 tbsp cider vinegar
1 tsp salt

Poach the fish in the water and vinegar with the onion and salt. Remove and keep hot. Add the currants and redcurrants to the pan and simmer for five minutes. Thicken with cornflour dissolved in a tablespoon of cold water. Arrange the fish in layers with the chopped prunes and dates and pour over the sauce.

A NOTE ON CONTEMPORARY RIVER FISH

Some fishmongers sell river fish and the most common is rainbow trout. It is perfectly legal to take fish from rivers as long as you have a rod license and the permission of the water owner. Common and edible river fish include bream, roach, rudd, tench, pike and perch.

✤ ROAST GOOSE

Geese were popular as birds that could glean the unenclosed fields, so ensuring no grain was wasted. Fattened in this way in the autumn they could then be killed for Christmas. Hence the anti-enclosure ditty above. This recipe originally dates from the late 14th century. Serves 4–6.

5–6 lb goose • 1 tsp parsley, chopped
1 tsp hyssop (bitter, minty leaves) • ½ tsp sage
½ tsp savoury
4 tbsp quince or crab apple jelly [see recipe p116]
2–3 pears, peeled, cored and chopped
1 clove garlic crushed
3 oz grapes, peeled and seeded
¼ pint jellied chicken stock
¼ pint red wine • ¼ tsp ginger • ½ tsp cinnamon
½ tsp nutmeg

Stuff the goose with the herbs, jelly, pears, garlic and seasoning to taste. Roast the goose in the oven on a rack in the roasting tray at 190°c/gas mark 5 allowing 15 minutes per lb and an extra 15 minutes. Geese have a lot of fat, so prick it all over with a fork and add some salt to the skin before putting it in the oven. Carve it and put the pieces and the stuffing in a sauté pan with the gravy and stock. Cook until reduced a little and add the wine and spices with salt to taste. Simmer for a few minutes until the wine has been absorbed and serve with roast potatoes and seasonal vegetables.

> **The fault is great in Man or Woman**
> **Who steals the Goose from off a Common;**
> **But who can plead that man's excuse**
> **Who steals the Common from the Goose?**

Iffley Manor and originally given to it by King Edward III, and a local farmer William Hurst, whose family have been described as 'one of the true yeoman families of England'. Their name lives on in Hurst Street.

In the early 18th century large parts of the country were still farmed in open fields, as they had been for centuries. But between 1750 and 1810 almost four thousand private Acts of Parliament were passed to authorise enclosures, as thousands of acres of common land were carved up into neat and tidy fields at the expense of the cottagers and day labourers who worked the strips in the common fields and grazed livestock on the common. With strip farming, each strip was about one third of an acre and was eight yards wide and a furlong or 'furrow long' i.e. 220 yards in length; the amount one person could plough in a day. This system whereby farmers cultivated many ridge and furrow strips widely scattered across open fields, 'strip farming', would constrain any building development because it would violate the common rights to pasture animals after the harvest on the open field stubble. A huge area cultivated in this way, stretched from Cowley village to the settlement in St Clement's and was known as Cowley Field. The ridge and furrow pattern associated with unenclosed fields are still clearly visible in the lower part of South Park, especially in early evening light.

These peasant farmers were also able to graze their pigs in the woods and forests further afield, a right known as 'pannage' i.e. on acorns, beech mast and the like. The colleges expected significant quantities of produce in return, especially at times of festivals. For example, The Queen's College had a 'Boar's Head Feast' on the Saturday before Christmas, a tradition that lasts to this day.

MAP 1: OXFORD CITY AND COWLEY ROAD

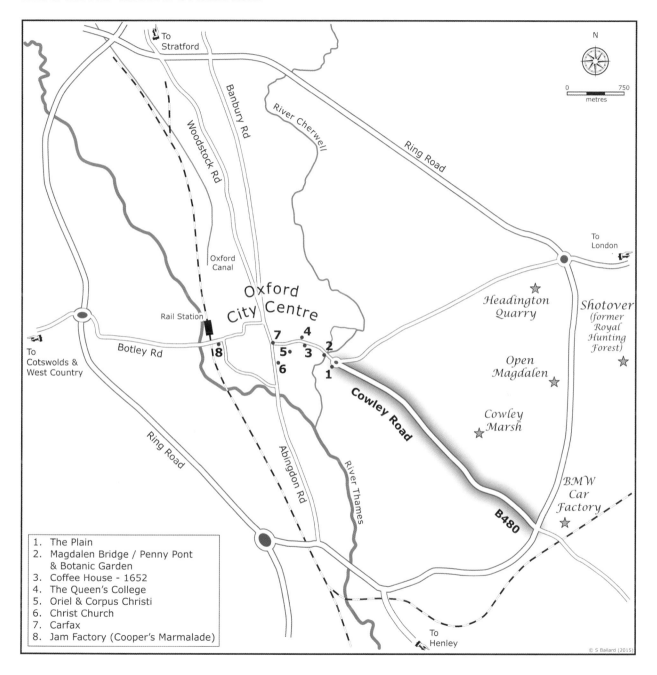

To Stratford

Banbury Rd

Woodstock Rd

River Cherwell

Ring Road

N

0 — 750
metres

To London

Oxford Canal

Oxford
City Centre

Headington
Quarry

Shotover
(former
Royal
Hunting
Forest)

Rail Station

7 4
2
8 5 3
6 1

Open
Magdalen

Botley Rd

To
Cotswolds &
West Country

Cowley Road

Cowley
Marsh

Ring Road

Abingdon Rd

River Thames

B480

BMW
Car
Factory

To Henley

© S Ballard (2015)

1. The Plain
2. Magdalen Bridge / Penny Pont
    & Botanic Garden
3. Coffee House - 1652
4. The Queen's College
5. Oriel & Corpus Christi
6. Christ Church
7. Carfax
8. Jam Factory (Cooper's Marmalade)

Population pressures and land values from a growing city meant that areas immediately around the City such as Marston and St Clement's, began to be enclosed from the middle of the 16th century. Pasture on either side of Headington Hill was enclosed in 1565. However, unusually, it was not until the 19th century that enclosure in east Oxford began to gather pace, with the enclosure of Headington parish in 1804.

Even so, Cowley parish remained unenclosed and strip-farmed in large open fields right up until the middle of the 19th century, with Bartholomew Field, Ridge Field (reflected in the street name Ridgefield Road) Lakes Field and Compass Field, which between them covered what is now thought of as east Oxford, all remaining unenclosed.

However, with industrialisation gathering pace across the country, enclosure was seen as necessary to feed a growing population more productively and profitably – 'improvement' as it was known to its advocates, and something had to give in the end.

But the landowners, the Oxford colleges, resisted the process because they valued and sought to preserve the open fields, including the fine turf on Cowley Marsh which was noted for its snipe and the uninterrupted distant views of the centre of Oxford. Christ Church in particular was opposed to enclosure because they thought land consolidation would lead to building on land that overlooked Christ Church Meadow.

As a result enclosure, despite the petitions of other landowners as early as 1821, was delayed. However, they were correct that enclosure was inevitable in east Oxford, and in anticipation, Christ Church planted a screen of trees along the west side of Iffley Road (which had been created as part of a road route to Henley in the 18th century) in 1852, wishing to preserve *a sense of what is best for the beauty of the entrance into Oxford*. Enclosure finally arrived in east Oxford the following year.

In the years following their defeat, the dons at Christ

Church probably consoled themselves with mock turtle soup immortalised by one of their number Charles Dodgson, better known as Lewis Carroll.

The size of the fields formed by enclosure varied, but they tended to be about ten acres. These fields formed the plots that were later sold on to developers and their varied shapes contributed to the layout of the many new streets constructed in east Oxford throughout the latter part of the 19th century. Their form was determined by the pre-existing routes passing through the area – the line of Cowley Road following the old drove road, running through east Oxford, up Barracks Lane and over Shotover Hill to London, while Iffley Road was the start of the route to Dorchester and Henley.

The combination of enclosure and the eastward growth of Oxford in the 19th century led to demands for space to grow food from those who had been deprived of their strips or had moved from the countryside to Oxford for work and were living in poor housing with inadequate wages. Strip farming was combined with open grazing on local commons and forest areas. One such was the Elderstub Coppice, first referred to in 1643 out near the Shotover Royal Hunting Forest. Parishioners of Cowley had rights of grazing, pannage and the collection of firewood 'by hook or by crook' i.e. no sawing or felling allowed, though this was often ignored. These grazing rights were maintained throughout the 19th century, but by the 1870s there were disputes, several of which ended up in court as parishoners had the habit of taking their cattle through a wooded area known as Open Magdalen (in the Wood Farm area), owned by Magdalen College and leased by Bartlemas farmer Richard Pether, who fenced and cleared part of the wood and erected a gate to keep them out. Local resistance was described as 'formidably protracted'.

The commons that stretched across large parts of east Oxford at this time gave variety to local people's diet, being described at the time as 'tremendous for mushrooms', and blackberries were abundant. So too were rabbits, netted in the autumn using ferrets. They took pride of place in a local hotpot called 'Shackles'. Raphael Samuel in his study of Headington Quarry and the surrounding area records that local people remembered dining off rabbit 'two or three times

MOCK TURTLE SOUP

Alice's Adventures in Wonderland include the Mock Turtle's story. 'Then the Queen . . ., said to Alice, "Have you seen the Mock Turtle yet?" "No" said Alice "I don't even know what a mock turtle is." "It's the thing mock turtle soup is made from" said the Queen "and he shall tell you his history."'
Mock Turtle soup was a substitute for green turtle soup which was made from real (and endangered) turtles. There are various cajun and other variations. Serves 6+.

8 tbsp vegetable oil • ¾ lb beef, cubed • ½ lb pork, cubed
7 oz flour • 1 large onion, chopped
4 spring onions, finely chopped
Several sprigs parsley, finely chopped
2 tbsp celery, finely chopped • 1 tsp dried thyme
4 pints beef broth (you can use stock cubes)
4 fl oz tomato sauce • Hot sauce to taste
½ lemon in wedges

Make up the beef broth. Heat the oil in a large heavy pan over a medium high heat. Add the meat and brown. Remove the meat and set aside. Cook the onions, spring onions, parsley and celery in the pan until the onions are translucent adding more oil if needed. Reduce the heat. Add the flour, stirring. Add two cups of the hot stock and stir to form a thick paste adding the tomato paste. Stir in the remaining stock, add the meats and hot sauce and salt to taste. Reduce the heat to low, cover and simmer for an hour. Cool slightly and skim off any excess fat. Serve with bread and a wedge of lemon.

❧ 'SHACKLES' OR RABBIT HOT-POT

'take taters, swedes, turnips and all that, rabbits. . .
couple of rabbits legs. . . all in together. . . that was nice
in winter. . . there waren't much left.'

Some added a 'bit o' bacon boiled with it, a few suety
dumplings. . . You had a real 'olesome dinner.'

My Irish grandmother had a very similar recipe for hare,
(see below) which involved jointing it and marinading
the meat for 12 hours in cider before cooking.

a week' in winter. One local resident, Fred Tolley is quoted
saying, *'It was our staple diet, nothing better'.*

GROWING BY THE PARISH LANTERN

After enclosure, and in compensation for the loss of grazing
rights on the Elder Stubbs coppice area of Shotover, the
'deserving labouring poor' of the Cowley parish were
allocated 16 acres of land to cultivate as allotments between
Cowley Road and Rymers Lane. It was a part of Cowley
Marsh and very prone to flooding. These are the Elder Stubbs
allotments of today and are still owned and let as allotments
by the successor charity. Individual allotments of 20 pole
were marked out and let on a tenancy agreement to suitable
parishioners at annual rents of about 10 shillings, around
a third of a labourer's weekly wage (roughly £175 a year in
modernday money). The loss of grazing, poaching, foraging,
pannage and firewood would have had a significant impact
on a labourer's household economy and allotment rent strikes
were common throughout the latter part of the 19th century.

Almost uniquely, a detailed diary has survived from this
period that was kept by one of those labourers, an allotment
holder named Joseph Turrill, who lived in Garsington just
outside Oxford. He rented an allotment in the village from the
estate owned by Oxford's leading brewing dynasty the Morrell
family, as well as using the garden of the Red Lion pub, where
his mother was licensee, to grow additional produce which
he sent to market in Oxford, mainly for the colleges. The
diary runs from 1863-67 and provides a vivid insight into
what crops plot holders at the time grew and the challenges,
particularly with the weather, that they faced in growing them.

Here is Turrill on the pleasures and pains of growing in
May and June 1863.

*'Wednesday. Hoed potatoes and earthed the peas up - don't
grow fast so cold and frosty nights and mornings*

*Saturday. Tied lettuce in gardens. . . cabbage want cutting
and lettuce wants pulling. . . a beautiful clear starlight night but
intensely cold and sharp white frost in the morning. Too cold for
nightingales. The blight among gooseberry trees is about again
but not bad at present, it is too cold. Had a swarm of bees on
Monday but it was very warm in the morning and they wanted*

to swarm before but the weather was so bad. Swarmed on a little gooseberry tree in front and went in the hive the first time very tidy and warm.

Sunday. The plum apple and damson trees seem set well and everything wants sun and warm weather. Planted 6 rows cabbage on Wednesday last 20 May 1863. Peas at bottom of lower Piece just coming up. Sharpened sticks for them.

Friday. Moulded potatoes in Common some time ago. [. . .] Tuesday 19 May '63. Made a cucumber bed on 27 May and planted 3 little plant from Ben Hanks. Peas in garden growing well. Mrs Wilgress buried May 29. Cream of tartar 1s 8d per pound. Budded roses on Friday 26 June. Dug first potatoes up on that day – yielded very tidy considering it be first lot. . . . Hoed the carrots among the cabbage the same day. All the cabbage and lettuce gone now.

June 27. Parsnips are blighting – peas are looking uncommonly well and onions. Here is a good prospect of apples, plums blackcurrants and potatoes. Rather dull weather now but fine. It rains now a little.

[. . .] Kidney beans just out in bloom. Ripe fruit coming in – raspberries, gooseberries, currants, strawberries etc. Apples on standard are large as a child's fist. Heard cuckoo today. . . .

July 7. Shallots nearly ripe and fruit ripening very fast – very hot dry weather indeed now – everything drying up for want of rain.

By August, harvest prospects were looking good. But the pressures of selling produce in Oxford and helping his mother in the pub meant the plots were often attended to by moonlight, known as the 'parish lantern'.

'Aug 1. The weather still continues very fine and warm now, 11 o'clock, the moon is shining very bright and not a cloud to be seen. I was down the common last night just finished gathering kidney beans when the church clock struck nine but it is getting quite dark now at that time. . . had the first ripe plums today. Wheat now gathered. Walnuts for pickling ourselves today. Sowed cabbage seed today about half an ounce but did not water it - sowed in drills. Gathered first apricots today in lower tree – about a dozen. . . . Nearly all the cabbage and lettuce gone. Harpers took up their potatoes

✥ PICKLED WALNUTS

Joseph Turrill may have left his pickling till early August but I don't recommend leaving it that late. Pickled walnuts use the entire fruit when it is still green, including the outer casing which turns black and falls off in the autumn revealing the ripe 'wet' walnuts. To pickle walnuts you need to catch them before the shell inside has begun to form and harden, generally no later than the end of June, or they will be completely inedible.

A couple of dozen green walnuts

Prick the walnuts all over with a long needle such as a carpet needle. Place in a large bowl or bucket and cover them in brine, 6 oz salt to 2 pints water, and leave for 5 days, stirring occasionally. Drain and cover with fresh brine for a further week. Drain, and set out on a tray in a sunny place for a day, turning occasionally.

When dry and black, pack into jars and cover with a spiced vinegar made as follows:
***3 pints malt vinegar • 1½ oz peppercorns • 1½ oz allspice
1 oz root ginger • Approx 1oz brown sugar to taste***

Add the sugar to the vinegar, put the spices in a muslin bag and place in the vinegar. Boil for ten minutes. Allow the vinegar to cool. Remove the spices. Pack the walnuts into jars, pour the liquid over them and close the jars. The pickled walnuts will be ready to eat in 6–8 weeks. They are very good with cheeses or cured meats such as ham. They can also be used in stews.

- good ones, 2 ½ bushel on Friday and Sunday. . . . He had a swarm of bees on Sunday, got stung.'

In discussing pickling walnuts, Ralph Ayres, head cook at New College in the early 18th century, recommended that you 'Gather then when they are a bout the bigness of a pigeons egge or before they have any shell'.

DIGGING FOR FOOD AND FREEDOM

Raphael Samuel who studied the 'free village' of Headington Quarry in the last quarter of the 19th century tells of a builder's labourer and navvy, William Green who was remembered by his son as having a large and productive garden,

'We had. . . fruit trees all down the centre. . . vegetables – potatoes and so on. . . pig sties half way down. . . hen houses. . . something of everything. . . we never bought vegetables.'

Another interviewee remembered the potato harvests of his childhood.

'The old man used to march us up there. I can hear him now when we were picking up 'taters. "Take 'em up don't tread the buggers in. . . ." We used to have a couple of days off school when we got the 'taters up. We used to borrow the old man's pony and cart to get them home. . . . We used to go up, mother and us boys, and dig up all day and when the old chap come home from work, he come straight up and load them up and away we come. Once we dug up the wrong plot – someone else's potatoes – and the old man come up at night; he swore but he took them round to the fellow. . . it ended all right.'

Demand for space to grow food rose during the First World War. In 1918, when the government belatedly introduced rationing after the success of the German U-boat campaigns from 1917 onwards, the Elder Stubbs trustees rented a further ten acres of land adjoining their Cowley site from Christ Church. The lease stipulated that the land was:

'not let as a Market Garden and no consent was given for. . . the planting of any orchards or fruit trees or bushes and further any asparagus, rhubarb or other perennial crop.'

Between the Wars allotments retained their importance as an essential support for a family's standard of living during the Depression. Garden historian Jenny Uglow, also saw a deeper impulse.

'Faced with the growing threat of fascism, digging the earth came to seem like a symbol of freedom and the vegetable garden a small world where one was in control, working with nature, free from politics.'

These days, about an acre of the Elder Stubbs site has been developed as an apple orchard. Planted in the early 1990s, there are 46 different apple varieties including rarities unavailable in any shop, such as the Pitmanston Pineapple.

Oxford as a whole is blessed with a large number of well-loved allotment sites, some 36 in all, of which 14 are in east Oxford and a further nine in Headington and Marston. These are mainly owned by the City Council and largely self-managed by allotment associations.

Allotments went through many vicissitudes after the enthusiasm engendered by the 'Dig for Victory' campaign during the Second World War, as living standards rose and the desire to 'grow your own' waned. Allotments went out of fashion, but Elder Stubbs Allotments, which are the only ones in the city run by a charitable trust, continue to thrive and remain to this day as one of the most enduring links between the past and the present in east Oxford.

CHAPTER TWO
'Parsons and sausages': Jam and beer

Oxford grew rapidly in the latter part of the 19th century, almost doubling in size between 1851 and 1901 to a population of just under 50,000. This was the time when Cowley Road and the streets running off it were laid out, developing gradually from the city end and the older buildings in St Clement's. After enclosure the fields were sold off to developers like the National Freehold Land Society. It bought land for Alma Place in 1852 and then acquired and laid out streets from Temple Street to Marston Street. The Hurst family, awarded a large area of land between James Street and Magdalen Road at enclosure, laid them out for housing in the early 1860s, although it took three decades for the area to be fully built up, while the area on the other side of Cowley Road, now Divinity Road and environs was developed from the early 1890s.

THE 'ROYAL' OXFORD SAUSAGE

Oxford was well placed in the centre of southern England as an agricultural centre. Farmers used the well-established drove roads to bring their animals to the city from as far away as Bristol for slaughter and it became something of a focus for meat processing. Inventive ways of preserving meat pre-refrigeration were developed, amongst them the 'Oxford sausage', made from a pork and veal recipe, which was invented in the 18th century by a Mrs Dorothy Spreadbury and caught on quickly. Ralph Ayres was serving a version to the dons of New College by the 1740s. By the late 19th century it had become very well known, not least by being popularised by Mrs Beeton in her book *Household Management* published in 1861, where she refers to it as her 'ideal sausage'. Such was its popularity that by the end of the century it had been transformed into the 'Royal Oxford sausage'.

The Piggott's sausage factory and associated abattoir which manufactured the Oxford sausage, were established in the 1880s in Denmark Street and local photographer and early Oxford publicist, Henry Taunt retells of an Oxford Alderman giving evidence to a Parliamentary Committee who made reference to 'Oxford manufacturers'.

'Alderman' asked one of the Hon members 'have you any manufactures at Oxford?" Oh yes sir' said the alderman 'we have two, parsons and sausages!'

✹ THE OXFORD SAUSAGE

Mrs Beeton used a 50/50 mix of pork and veal in her recipe. Traditionally it was considered to be a 'breakfast sausage' and is notably spicy. The recipe doesn't need skins because of the beef suet which stiffens it. Roll it in flour instead before frying. This is the 'modern version' i.e. without veal.

2 lbs good quality lean pork, such as shoulder
1 lb beef suet · 1 lb breadcrumbs
Rind of ½ a lemon, finely grated · 6 fresh sage leaves
Grating of nutmeg or mace · ½ tsp of dried marjoram
1 tsp of savoury herbs to hand · Salt and pepper

Chop or mince the pork and suet finely together. Add the breadcrumbs and lemon peel and a grating of nutmeg. Wash and chop the sage leaves finely. Add these with the remaining ingredients to the sausage mix and when thoroughly mixed roll into sausages, cut to desired lengths and roll in flour. These can be eaten with horseradish sauce and celeriac and potato [see recipe p93] as a main meal.

A NOTE ON SUET. Suet is beef fat and was commonly available when whole carcases were delivered to butchers. However it is now more difficult to find and is sold as the brand 'Atora'. However even this is no longer common. Some butchers e.g. Alders sell the original which needs to be sliced or grated, around Christmas time, mainly for the making of Christmas puddings.

✹ MARMALADE-GLAZED SAUSAGES

For the authentic 'Oxford signature dish', add a marmalade glaze to the sausages by taking (for six sausages) 3 tbsp marmalade warming it in a pan adding anything else you may wish e.g. caramelised onion, or a little cider vinegar, and spreading the sauce over the (cooked) sausages in a pan. Return the sausages to the oven at 180°c/gas mark 4 for 15 minutes to allow the marmalade glaze to bake. Shake the sausages around to make sure that they are fully covered with the glaze. Serve in French bread with optional mustard or ketchup.

Local people were less forgiving and regularly complained of the smell. One elderly local resident Bert Silvester told me he still remembers it from his daily walk to school as a child, but it remained open until 1937.

Alden's ('est. 1793') who still have a shop in the Covered Market were at one point the largest butchers in England and they reared cattle, sheep, and pigs for local consumption at Eastwyke Farm off Abingdon Road. Being a livestock centre meant that grain was also an important commodity. The Corn Exchange was on the ground floor of the Town Hall until it was re-built in 1894 when it moved to purpose-built premises on George Street, now the Old Fire Station Arts Centre. The Corn Exchange sign carved in stone is still visible on the front of the building.

PARSONS

East Oxford had a long religious tradition, from the days of the monks offering sanctuary, hospitality and healing at Bartlemas in the 13th century. Divinity Walk, roughly along the line of the current Divinity Road, was a well-known place for clerics to exercise and read scriptures in a rural setting from the early 18th century onward, and in the 19th century, the area became a significant centre for religious orders as the suburb grew. Many were dissenting and found the restrictions of the University with its Anglican tradition, onerous. As religious communities they retained that tradition of hospitality for pilgrims and help for the sick and vulnerable seeking both simplicity and a certain level of self-sufficiency. Many were keen horticulturalists. One such community was the Society of St John the Evangelist, the first religious community in the Anglican Church. Founded in 1866 by the Rev RM Benson it became known locally as the 'Cowley Fathers'. They settled on a site between the Cowley and Iffley Roads, bounded by Marston Street and James Street, in 1868. They remained there for over 100 years. They were keen on a connection with the earth and growing their own food was an important part of community life. The Cowley Fathers cultivated a large vegetable garden, a potato plot, a fruit cage, a large greenhouse and an orchard with a brick-built apple store with wooden shelving for storing the fruit. There was a large lawn at the centre of the community and a huge mulberry tree in the middle of the cloister with blackberries along its outside wall. The community's last head gardener was the appropriately named Fr Alan Bean, who was also a nationally recognised expert on bees. The Cowley Fathers finally relinquished the site, now St Stephen's House, in 1980.

OXFORD MARMALADE

The sausage apart, probably the best known of Oxford's foods is Frank Cooper's Oxford Marmalade.

Cooper inherited a business on the High St in 1867 and his wife Sarah, started marmalade production in 1874 by selling 73 lbs of her own home made marmalade from the premises.

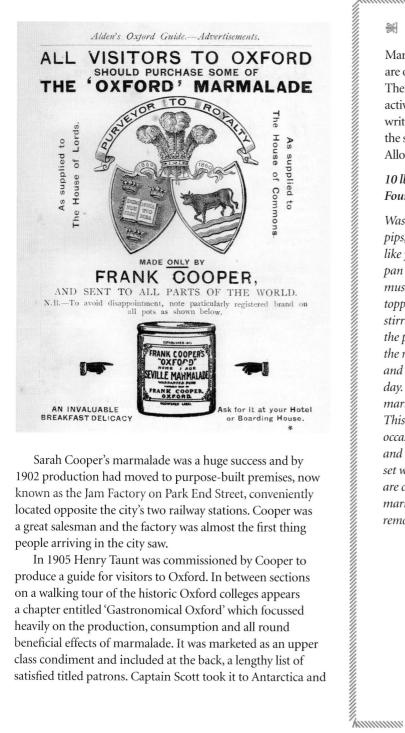

Sarah Cooper's marmalade was a huge success and by 1902 production had moved to purpose-built premises, now known as the Jam Factory on Park End Street, conveniently located opposite the city's two railway stations. Cooper was a great salesman and the factory was almost the first thing people arriving in the city saw.

In 1905 Henry Taunt was commissioned by Cooper to produce a guide for visitors to Oxford. In between sections on a walking tour of the historic Oxford colleges appears a chapter entitled 'Gastronomical Oxford' which focussed heavily on the production, consumption and all round beneficial effects of marmalade. It was marketed as an upper class condiment and included at the back, a lengthy list of satisfied titled patrons. Captain Scott took it to Antarctica and

✄ OXFORD MARMALADE

Marmalade making involves using Seville oranges, which are only available in the shops in January and February. Therefore I consider marmalade making to be an annual activity and so I make a year's supply at once. Some cookery writers seem to think ordinary oranges are OK. They aren't the same at all. This recipe will make about two dozen jars,. Allow most of a day to make this quantity.

10 lbs Seville oranges • Four sweet oranges
Four unwaxed lemons • 10 lbs Demerara sugar

Wash the fruit. Quarter it and then carefully remove the pips, retaining them all. Slice up all the fruit as finely as you like your marmalade. Place the fruit into a large preserving pan with at least three litres of water. Put the pips in a muslin bag and put them in the pan. Cook for two hours, topping up with water as you go along if necessary and stirring to ensure the fruit doesn't stick to the bottom of the pan. The fruit can be left overnight at this point. When the rinds are soft and the mix is reduced, remove the pips and add the sugar – slowly. This can be done the following day. Stir well, bring to the boil and keep stirring until the marmalade begins to set. Keep a close eye on progress. This is likely to take at least an hour. Test by removing the occasional spoonful placing it on a plate, allowing it to cool and checking how well it has set with your finger. It has set when the cooled juice wrinkles. Make sure your pots are clean and dry and warm them in the oven or the hot marmalade will crack them. When the marmalade is ready, remove from the heat, fill and seal the jars. Allow to cool.

Opposite: Oxford Co-operative
Society bread delivery in east
Oxford, 1924.

Inside Cooper's Oxford
Marmalade factory, *c.*1910.

Frank Cooper's imposing
Marmalade factory opposite
Oxford rail stations, *c.*1910.

Kim Philby insisted on a regular supply after his defection to Moscow, supplied by the KGB.

Marmalade is the ultimate breakfast condiment, particularly in Oxford. However its popularity has declined; it is apparently considered to be 'old fashioned', although the release of the children's film *Paddington*, featuring a well-known marmalade-eating bear, in 2014 may aid a revival in interest.

Cooper's marmalade manufacture was inevitably seasonal and he branched out into a range of other potted products including mint sauce, gentleman's relish and perhaps best known of all, horseradish sauce.

BREAD AND BEER

As the city population grew in the 19th century 'town versus gown' tensions over food were never far below the surface, as the colleges exerted significant buying power as well as being major local landowners. Not surprisingly they obtained foodstuffs at favourable rates as a result, and the last recorded bread riot in the city occurred in 1867 when a leading corn merchant Isaac Grubb, was accused by townspeople of selling bread to the colleges more cheaply than he did to the ordinary paying public. He was only too well aware of his ambiguous status in the eyes of townspeople; he had an outlet on St Clements as well as supplying the colleges, and sought to head off hostility in 1887 by celebrating Queen Victoria's Golden Jubilee with a much advertised cut in his bread and flour prices.

❧ HORSERADISH SAUCE

The plants are commonly found in Oxford from days when it was grown semi-commercially to supply Frank Cooper's operation. It is large, with slightly toothed dock-like foliage and grows to about 3 ft. Dig down deep; the roots are long.

To prepare, peel it down to the white inner root. It is quite strongly flavoured.

1 oz freshly grated horseradish root
(approx 2–3 heaped tbsp)
½ pint yoghurt or double cream
1 tsp dry mustard
1 tsp sugar
Salt and pepper

Mix together and allow to stand for 15 minutes.

Serve with beef, venison, or the Oxford Sausage, and as an accompaniment to celeriac and potato [see recipe p93] or as an alternative topping for soups instead of crème fraiche.

It keeps in the fridge for about 3–4 days before losing its flavour.

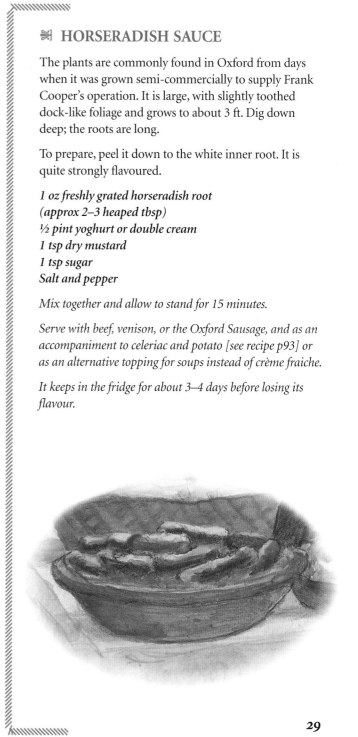

Roy Gibbons and Gibbons Bakery, Hertford Street.

Bakeries and other shops to supply local demand were to be found in practically every street at this time and were often established in the front rooms of houses where food was produced. They were frequently on street corners and can be recognised by their distinctive large rectangular ground floor windows and sometimes the house name e.g. The Old Dairy in Denmark St.

Phyl Surman in her book *Pride of the Morning* recalls being brought up on Howard Street in the 1920s and 30s. Bread, fish, meat, milk, fruit and vegetables could all be bought from small shops in the immediate locality, or from door to door salesmen.

'*Bread came round in horse drawn vans, not wrapped or sliced but crusty and golden brown fresh from the oven for there were no big multiple bakers and baking was all done locally by small firms. . . Fresh fish and rabbits were also brought round the streets by horse and cart transport . . . Local farmers delivered milk in large tinned steel churns to various small dairies throughout Oxford: our nearest was the Oxford Dairy in Little Percy Street and from here the delivery men would set out, each with a small truck carrying one or two churns, crying as they went "Milk-O".*'

One of the shops Surman was referring to was Hudson's Bakery in Hertford Street, which opened in 1894. One hundred and twenty years later it is still open, now called Gibbons Bakery and the proprietors Roy and Diane Gibbons who have run it since 1981, still deliver bread locally.

Local traders were very much part of people's daily lives and stories of their antics abound. Roy Gibbons recalls that Hudson's was for many years run by a baker called 'Tiddley' Lambourn who delivered bread by horse and cart and was a well-known drinker. He regularly got so drunk that he fell into the cart, but the horse knew to bring him back to the bakery. He was killed at the very end of the Second World War when a tank transporter transporting Crusader tanks – which were manufactured at the Cowley car plant from 1942 as part of the War effort – accidentally backed into the pony and trap while he lay unconscious inside. The War had a big effect on delivery businesses like Hudson's because of lack of fuel which was rationed or sold on the black market, which meant they could no longer operate economically and that, combined with the arrival of discount shops on Cowley Road like Butler's, (which started out in the 1880s as a corn merchant and bakery) gradually put all the other bakeries in east Oxford out of business.

Such is the reputation of Gibbon's bread, that the shop was a finalist in the BBC Food and Farming Awards in 2000.

For Surman in the 1920s, Cowley Road meant sophistication and excitement. At the bottom of the road

'... near to the fountain and facing Magdalen College School stood a coffee cabin, a wooden vehicle the side flap of which lifted up to form a canopy revealing counter rows of thick white mugs and "doorsteps" of bread and cheese. During cold weather by means of a coke stove whose chimney protruded through a roof of the vehicle, supplies of hot steaming tea and coffee were brewed and the slopping cups slid onto the narrow counter where they were gratefully grasped by hands blue and trembling with cold.'

The Victoria Drinking Fountain which is still in place at the bottom of Cowley Road, was inaugurated on 25 May 1899 by Princess Louise and was sponsored by the Morrell's of Headington Hill Hall.

The Morrell family were the dominant brewing family in the City for over 150 years. They built Headington Hill Hall in 1824 which is now part of Oxford Brookes University and was notoriously the home of newspaper tycoon Robert Maxwell in the 1970s and 80s. Morrell Avenue, running up the side of South Park, itself donated to the City by the Morrell family in the 1930s, commemorates the link. At the time their Lion Brewery on St Thomas Street closed in 2002, they had over 130 'tied' pubs in Oxford.

A 'drink map' of Oxford published in 1875 shows over 300 pubs, though east Oxford was relatively poorly supplied, partly because the area was being developed as a respectable suburb and partly because the main breweries were in the west of the City, heavily concentrated in St Thomas parish near the station – and so were the pubs. Both the canal which arrived in 1790 and the railway in 1844, encouraged the growth of brewing and by 1875 there were eight main commercial breweries in the city. Only one was in east Oxford; St Clement's Brewery in Little Brewery St, established in 1826 and later known as Wootten's Brewery, operated by Wootten and Co.

In 1920 Cowley Road had one brewer, six pubs and a 'beer retailer', two fish and chip shops and a tearoom. There were also no less than thirty three food shops, of which seven were butchers, six greengrocers and fruiterers, four confectioners and two each were bakers and fishmongers. Liptons, Home & Colonial and the Co-op were also represented. One of the confectioners conveniently had an artificial teeth manufacturer located next door.

❧ GIBBONS BAKERY COTSWOLD CRUNCH BREAD

I don't make bread all that much because I like the bread baked round the corner from my house by Roy and Diane Gibbons in the bakery in Hertford Street. But here is a recipe that draws upon their 'Cotswold crunch' loaf. Grown and milled in the Cotswolds you can buy the flour from Gibbons too. This bread really does make great toast to have for breakfast. It is equally delicious cut thick with cheese, spreads and salad.

500 g Cotswold crunch – a mixture of strong white flour, malt flour and malted wheat flakes
10 g fresh yeast or 1 tsp dried yeast
1 tsp salt
1 tsp brown sugar
2 tbsp sunflower oil
300 ml warm water

Pour 100 ml of the warm water into a small bowl, stir in the sugar and sprinkle the yeast into it. Leave for 10 minutes for the yeast to dissolve and froth. In a large bowl mix the flour and salt and rub in the oil, making sure it is evenly distributed through the flour. Pour the yeasty water into the flour and add most of the rest of the water. Knead the dough until it is smooth, perhaps five minutes or so and leave in the bowl covered with a damp cloth to rise. Depending on how warm the kitchen is this will take 1–2 hours. It should double in size. When it has, knock it down and knead again until light, again about five minutes. Press the dough into a couple of lightly-greased baking tins. Cover again and leave to double in size, which this time should only take 20–30 minutes.

While the dough is 'proving', pre-heat the oven to 230°c/ gas mark 8 and bake them for about 35 minutes.

When cooked the loaves should sound hollow when the bottom is tapped. Allow to cool before eating.

Jack Buckler's Christmas turkey display *c*.1928.

Christmas time was always one when Surman enjoyed the variety of Cowley Road:

'*The main shopping area in Cowley Road was lined with stores whose tinselled trappings glistened and sparked in the fluttering gaslight. There seemed to be an abundance of everything: pyramids of fruit, crates of vegetables: and above the poulterer's shop window rows of plucked turkeys geese and other fowl were suspended by their feet. . . . We mingled with other shoppers heavily laden with bulky parcels Christmas trees and here and there a straw bag from which protruded on the one side the trussed feet and on the other the bored, dead face of a turkey.*'

As the east Oxford suburbs grew, with the construction amongst others of the Florence Park Estate in 1934, Cowley Road became a more established and independent shopping centre distinct from the retail concentration in the city centre. Even after the Second World War local greengrocers and corner shops remained a typical sight in any city. But there were larger retailers too. The Oxford and District Co-op Society was one of the more ambitious and operated from the Co-op Arcade which opened in 1909, whose outlets included a butcher, grocer, chemist, gentleman's outfitter, furnishing shop, shoe shop and at the entrance, a greengrocers.

But the Co-op lost out to competition from Tesco in the 1970s and became a shadow of its former self before finally closing in 1982. The Co-op Hall upstairs remained as a venue for political meetings and for the use of youth groups like the Co-op affiliated Woodcraft Folk for a further decade before being sold and converted into a rock venue, the Zodiac and later the O2 Academy.

By the end of the 1940s the supermarket revolution was on its way from America. As with many other food-related trends to come, Cowley Road was a pace-setter. Returning from a trip to the USA in 1950, Bobby Silk inspired by what he saw there, established the first supermarket in Oxford, 'Silks Self-service Stores' in 1951, converting his existing

grocers business on the corner of Rectory Road. Silk was Jewish and knew Jack Cohen, founder of the Tesco chain. Cohen apparently promised Silk that he would not set up a competing store on Cowley Road while Silk was still trading. In the end Tesco opened in 1962, but another local supermarket, Butler's, was already well established when Tesco finally arrived. Advertisements appeared in the local press in July 1962 promoting the 'brand new money saving Tesco Supermarket'. The shop was open for family shopping nights every Friday until 7.30 pm and stocked over 4,000 branded lines. Nowadays trading is from 6am to midnight six days a week and there are 17,000 lines in stock. It grew with a modernisation upgrade in 1970, expanding to take in its rival Butler's and now trades as Tesco Metro, occupying a strategic chunk of Cowley Road, very conveniently backing directly onto the City Council-run public car park.

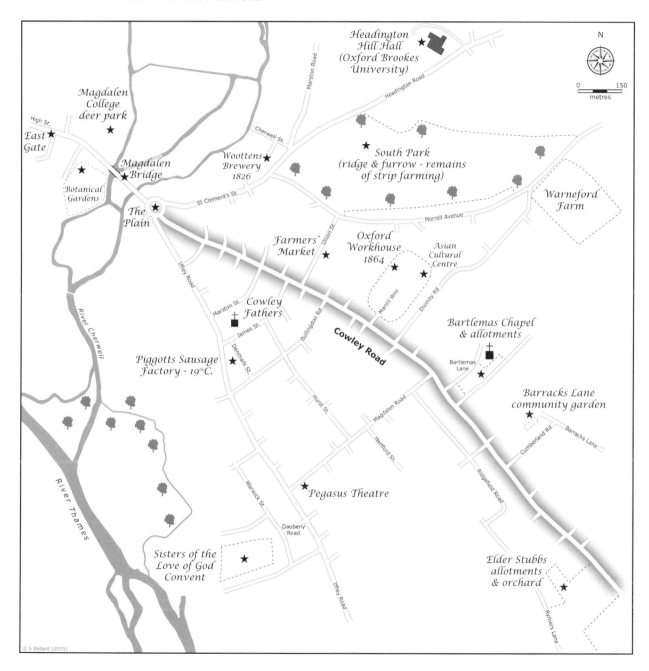

N

0   150
metres

Headington
Hill Hall
(Oxford Brookes
University)

Marston Road

Headington Road

Magdalen
College
deer park

Cherwell St.

High St.

East
Gate

South Park
(ridge & furrow - remains
of strip farming)

Warneford
Farm

Magdalen
Bridge

Woottens
Brewery
1826

St Clement's St.

Morrell Avenue

Botanical
Gardens

The
Plain

Farmers'
Market

Union St.

Oxford
Workhouse
1864

Asian
Cultural
Centre

Manzil Way

Divinity Rd

Iffley Road

River Cherwell

Marston St.

Cowley
Fathers

James St.

Bullingdon Rd

Cowley Road

Bartlemas Chapel
& allotments

Bartlemas
Lane

Piggotts Sausage
Factory - 19ᵗʰ C.

Denmark St.

Hurst St.

Magdalen Road

Barracks Lane
community garden

Cumberland Rd

Barracks Lane

River Thames

Hertford St.

Ridgefield Road

Warwick St.

Pegasus Theatre

Daubeny
Road

Iffley Road

Elder Stubbs
allotments
& orchard

Sisters of the
Love of God
Convent

Rymers Lane

© S Ballard (2015)

33

CHAPTER THREE

From the Caribbean to Capri

The competition between the supermarkets and established outlets like the Co-op was not the only story of changing food shopping on Cowley Road. The traditional shops such as fishmongers, fruiterers, bakers and butchers were squeezed by the convenience and low prices of supermarkets, but these themselves were reflecting changing consumer habits. The end of rationing in June 1954 following the shortages of war time, the arrival of fridges in the home and the more widespread ownership of the motor car – including the Morris marque made just up the road at Cowley – allowed people to shop less frequently and to buy more at one time.

East Oxford historian Annie Skinner records that in a typical year in the 1950s there were nine 'eating houses and take away restaurants', ten confectioners, five pubs, three wine and beer stores and no less than 36 food stores including butchers, grocers, fruiterers and bakers on Cowley Road. At their peak there were no fewer than seven butchers along the road between Marston Street and Randoph Street.

Just one, Alder's, still survives on the corner of Randolph Street. Andy Alder is the proprietor and the shop has been in the family since 1938, although there has been a butcher's shop on the site since 1903. As the last remaining independent butcher on Cowley Road, Alder's has a clientele who appreciate their local sourcing, free range meat and organic specialisms. This includes a large number of local restaurants including (at the time of writing) Hi-Lo, Door 74, The Rusty Bicycle, The Magdalen Arms and Beetroot.

While trade with local restaurants and families keep the shop thriving, the increase in the number of students is a concern as they don't use the shop, largely relying on eating out and prepared meals – trends that are becoming more widespread in Andy's view.

There were three fishmongers: one Harry Slater's (no 3) near The Plain which also supplied some of the Oxford colleges with game closed in 1983; one Byard's at 171 on the corner of Chapel St which was a subsidiary of Byard's in the Covered Market, and J Buckler and Son at 168 Cowley Road.

Jack Buckler opened his fishmonger and poulterer shop in 1907 having learned his trade from his father Sam who has a

✄ HAND OF PORK

This is Andy Alder's favourite – must be a winner being recommended by a butcher. The fat in the skin gives a great flavour. Hand of pork is a relation of the uber-trendy 'pulled pork', so beloved of a certain kind of restaurant. That recipe involves an overnight marinade, similar cooking times and served, typically in pitta bread with coleslaw. This far superior approach to the meat serves 6–7.

3 kg hand of pork on the bone (basically the front leg)
Butter • Salt

Score the skin, brush with butter and sprinkle thickly with salt.

Place in baking tin in a hot oven 220°c/gas mark 8, for 5–10 minutes.

Reduce the temperature to 180°/gas mark 4 and set to roast. Allow an hour per kilo.

Serve with roast potatoes, root vegetables, apple sauce and sage and onion stuffing. Don't expect to carve the joint. Pull the meat off with kitchen tongs.

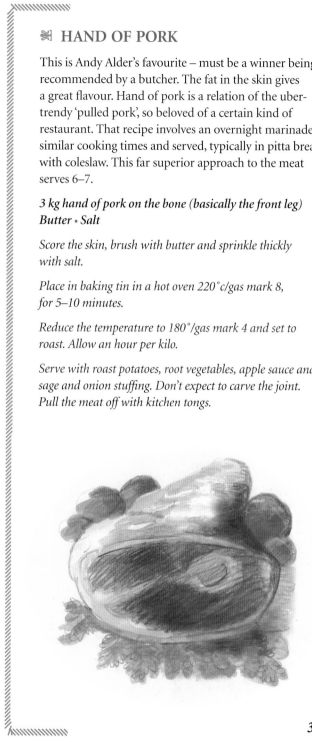

Chopping meat at Andy Alder's butchers (right); Andy Alder (below).

fishmonger's shop in the city centre. He ran it until 1936 when his son Stan took it over. They employed a night watchman at Christmas time when the sheer volume of stock meant that he left the poultry and rabbits hanging outside overnight.

Stan was joined by a young man, Gordon Thompson, in 1956. Thompson was a chef at Magdalen College and living round the corner in Hawkins Street. Thompson recalls that the offer from Stan to join the business came out of the blue in the bar of the Conservative Club. The shop was struggling but Thompson was a local activist and said: *'It soon looked up because so many people knew me and came into the shop to chat and buy.'* The shop was traditional in nature with an open front and the local environmental health inspector took exception to it.

Thompson recalls how he was able to prove that the fish on the slabs was cooler than those in the fridge (the visit was in November). He liked the open front because:

'There was lots of friendly gossip and you were closer to your customers. Six months after the health inspector's visit, I was elected to the City Council and I didn't get any more hassle after that.'

He served ten years as a Conservative councillor for St Clements. Apart from early closing on Thursdays he took no holidays, although once he was on the council he also closed on the Mondays of full council meetings: *'Mondays were never a big fish day.'* Throughout his time at the shop Thompson recalls that the fish came by rail from Grimsby and Hull and there was a delivery every day.

'It was all white fish or smoked fish, cod, haddock – my favourite – herrings, mackerel and some trout and prawns. No salmon, too expensive, or tuna, not available in those days.'

Thompson ran the shop on his own after Stan Buckler died, finally closing in 1990.

COWLEY ROAD'S ETHNIC ROOTS

The arrival of ethnic shops, cafés and restaurants on Cowley Road and laying their roots for success is the street's most distinctive and celebrated feature. In 2015 there were some 63 food shops, cafés and restaurants between the Plain and Magdalen Road, with a further 13 further up Cowley Road or in the streets around, particularly on Magdalen Road. The range is extraordinary, including Indian, Middle Eastern, Italian, Nepalese, Afghan, Persian, Chinese, Korean, Russian, Greek, Polish, Lebanese, Bangladeshi, Jamaican, Turkish, Moroccan, American, Japanese, Thai, Vietnamese, Algerian and Spanish. They come and go with almost bewildering speed. One premises has in the year I have spent writing this book, been successively Brazilian, Albanian and Lebanese. Add to this various 'fusion' food styles and of course, British cuisine and Cowley Road has a range of styles and traditions probably unrivalled on a single street anywhere else in Britain.

But why did this happen on Cowley Road? In part this was an unintended consequence of attempts from the end of the Second World War to adjust the actual physical form of the city to what the civic and University leaders of the time thought it ought to be.

From the Second World War onwards, east Oxford, which had until then been seen as a charming working class suburb, was viewed as much less desirable. The reason was that post-War, major plans were hatched for the City, the most ambitious of which was essentially to create two adjoining cities, an historic Oxford of the colleges, frozen in time, and a new suburban and industrial city east of the Thames based around the car factories which had sprung up after the First World War thanks to the entrepreneurship of William Morris, later Lord Nuffield. Cowley Road was to become its hub, with civic buildings including a new town hall, museum and library moving to sites on the street. This was to be combined with a major new shopping centre, the Cowley Centre, further out serving the yet-to-be-built outer housing estates such as Blackbird Leys. The plan was partly realised: both Blackbird Leys and the Cowley Centre were built, but the city remained as one. Instead, plans to protect the historic city centre focussed on getting the traffic out of the city rather than the people.

Over the following decades there were two road proposals aimed at achieving this, the 'Meadows Road' running across Christ Church Meadows and following a huge outcry against this despoliation of the historic setting of the city, an alternative further out, known as the 'Eastwyke Farm Road'.

❦ GORDON THOMPSON'S FRIED HADDOCK AND CHIPS

When a fishmonger offers you a recipe for fish, you take notice. *'The less you mess about with fish the better'* was his motto. So this makes a good, simple, traditional, east Oxford working class meal. Serves 4

4 x 180 g haddock or cod fillets • 1 tbsp plain flour
4 ripe tomatoes sliced • 2 eggs, beaten • 400 g chipping potatoes 1.5 l sunflower oil • Salt and pepper to taste

Roll the fish fillets in a mixture of the flour salt and pepper. Shake off excess flour. Set aside. Fill a large pan half full with the oil. Heat. Slice the potatoes into long slender chips and dry well in absorbent kitchen paper. When the oil is hot but not burning, drop the chips in a few at a time, so as to make sure the oil doesn't cool too much. When cooked through but not browned remove and drain. Meanwhile dip the fish in the beaten egg, coat with flour and fry in a pan with oil and the sliced tomatoes. Soften the tomatoes, brown both sides of the fish and remove. Place in a hot oven. Return the chips to the oil and cook for a few seconds. Remove and serve the fish with the chips, green vegetable of choice, traditionally peas, (but beans or broccoli are good) and ketchup.

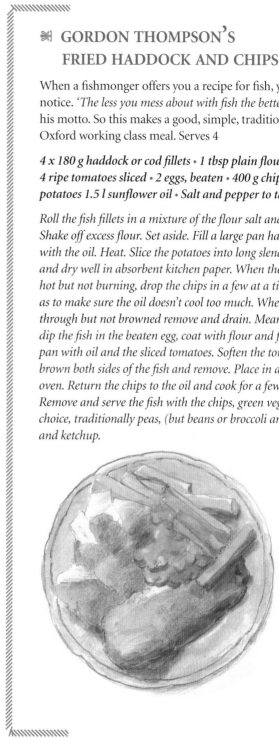

Gordon Thompson in his fish shop in the 1980s.

These proposals both involved running major roads though east Oxford with the inevitable substantial demolition and remodelling of the streetscape around Cowley Road; the intention being that new ring road round the old city would link to the London Road and a route down to London. These plans were first mooted in the mid 1940s and the final abandonment of the Eastwyke Farm Road plan was not until 1978. This combination of proposed compulsory purchase for both of the road proposals and the new civic centre and potential disruption to the urban form as a result of a major urban motorway carving through the neighbourhood, led to decades of 'planning blight'. There followed the inevitable decay of properties and streetscape right along the length of Cowley Road and in the surrounding area. However, the depressed housing and commercial property market in the area were also an opportunity for those prepared to take the risk.

REFUGEES OF THE ROAD: DELIS AND DEMOLITION

So where did the culinary revolution of Cowley Road start? British delis serving 'foreign foods' were a presence on Cowley Road from the 1940s, but the first ethnic food shop was Frank Harper & Son known locally as 'Eddie's', a shop run by a Polish refugee which opened in 1966 and described as a 'delicatessen', on the corner of Bullingdon Road.

Post-war refugees from Eastern Europe particularly Poles, Serbs and Russians were drawn to Oxford by its booming economy, along with Greek, Turkish and Italian communities, and a substantial Irish presence, all attracted by ready employment in the car factories and associated engineering firms. They were soon joined by both Afro-Caribbean and Asian communities who also came to work on the buses and in the hospitals, during the 1950s and 60s. They gravitated to the area (though the Asian community originally settled in the Jericho/Walton Street and west Oxford areas) partly because of its proximity to jobs, but also because of cheap housing, a result of the 'planning blight'. Bartlemas Chapel came into its own again after centuries of neglect, serving as a church and social focal point for the refugee Orthodox community until 1949, before moving to Marston Street where it stayed until 1973.

This ethnic diversity was soon reflected in the shops and cafés along Cowley Road. The traditional fish and chip shops such as Simon Fish and Chips dates from these immediate post war days. It is still trading. Establishments such as Mike's Café, Sid's Café, the Oak Tree Café and Fullbrook Farm Restaurant, remembered locally as *'a kind of milkshake bar with pictures of cows on the walls'*, were joined in 1960 by the first Chinese restaurant, the Kumling, followed by a second, the Pagoda in 1962. The first Indian restaurant, the Himalay also opened in 1962. At this time Indian restaurants were still rare outside London. Oxford had just one other, the Taj Mahal in Turl Sreet. It opened in 1937 and is reputed to be the first outside London. It survived until 2010.

CAPRESE CONNECTIONS

It was at this time that the Italian community began to make its presence felt on Cowley Road. The first Italian restaurant, La Capannina, opened in 1966, run by Giuseppe 'Joe' and Anna Arcucci who lived over the restaurant. They were Caprese and had arrived from Capri in the mid 1950s. They moved to Oxford from London to work at 'Fantasia,' the coffee bar in Queen Street, but were always on the lookout for a business of their own and took on the lease when the Fullbrook Farm Restaurant closed. Their daughter Carmelina, who worked in the restaurant from the age of 12 remembers the early days.

La Capannina, 1995.

✖ OSSOBUCO MILANESE

This is really a slow braised veal recipe and the bone doesn't actually have a hole in it. Rather, it is full of marrow and is the dish's crowning glory. Joe and Anna served Ossobuco Milanese for many years with plain rice and mushrooms. This is a home recipe which has also been updated by reference to British food writer Felicity Cloake's version. Serves 4.

4 pieces of veal shin, each about 4 cms thick
1 onion, finely chopped • 1 carrot, finely chopped
1 celery stick, finely chopped
1 large clove of garlic, cut horizontally • 2 strips lemon zest
4 sage leaves • 2 tbsp olive oil • 50 g butter • 25 g flour to dust
200ml white wine • 200ml chicken stock
Risotto rice (carnaroli) for four, infused with saffron

For the gremolata garnish: *1 unwaxed lemon zest, finely grated • 1 garlic clove, finely chopped • 3 tbsp flat leaf parsley, finely chopped • Pinch of sea salt*

Place a casserole dish large enough to hold the meat in one layer over a high heat and add the oil. Put the flour on a small plate, season generously and use this to coat the meat. When the oil is hot add the meat to the pan and brown well on both sides until golden and crusted. Set aside on a plate. Turn down the heat and add most of the butter to the pan. When melted add the onion, carrot and celery and a little salt and cook until soft. Add the garlic halves, lemon zest and sage and cook for a few more minutes. Turn up the heat and add the wine. Return the meat placing it on top of the vegetables and simmer until the wine is reduced by half. Pour in the stock and return to simmer. Turn the heat right down, cover the pan and simmer for 1½ hours carefully turning the meat over every 30 minutes. Cook until it is tender enough to cut with a spoon; simmer a little longer if necessary. Add the remaining butter and allow it to melt into the sauce. Cook the risotto rice. Mix the gremolata garnish ingredients together.

'The area was pretty run down, but my parents thought the location had potential because it was opposite the Regal Cinema with a ready source of customers. When we opened you couldn't buy a pepper and nobody knew what an aubergine was. There was no easy access to Mediterranean ingredients.'

The restaurant soon developed its own style attracting a loyal crowd of local people, both residents and a lunchtime trade from local businesses. Tastes were conservative.

'We were catering for the English market. The British palate required their food to be heavily sauced. We served an Italian version of meat and two veg.'

Top favourites were steak pizzaiola, steak done in tomato, garlic and oregano sauce served with spaghetti, and various escalopes, a kind of wiener schnitzel base, covered in a white sauce. For the more adventurous ossobuco, literally a bone with a hole in it, was the speciality of choice.

The food was served in a restaurant whose decor remained unchanged from when it first opened until Joe and Anna retired in 2006; all dark wood, raffia-clad wine bottles, strings of garlic and salamis hanging from the bar and the wooden beams. La Capannina was a great favourite of my children when they were small and was nicknamed 'the wooden restaurant'.

La Capannina; all raffia-clad wine bottles, strings of garlic and wooden beams.

La Capaninna was the sheet anchor of an Italian community that went on to open up plenty of other restaurants in Oxford such as Luna Caprese in north Oxford and Mario's along Cowley Road. Almost all of these restaurateurs worked with Joe and Anna at some point and a large proportion were Caprese.

As the Caribbean community in east Oxford grew, Eddie was approached by members of the community, to see if he would stock West Indian food. He agreed, and soon his shop took off as a West Indian place, selling sweet potatoes, okra and other specialist Caribbean foods. By the early 1970s he sold almost exclusively Afro-Caribbean foods. One regular customer recalls that the atmosphere was very relaxed and Eddie would often go to the Ampney Cottage, the pub across the road for a pint, park himself in a window seat and when a customer went into his shop return to serve them. The Ampney Cottage itself was transferred to an Afro-Caribbean landlord, Patrick 'Junior' Lennon in 1981.

EXCELSIOR CAFÉ: 'OPEN UNTIL 10.40 PM'

Although an ostensibly British 'greasy spoon', the Excelsior Café which was opened in 1955 was very much an international café in outlook by the early 1960s, daringly advertising itself as 'open until 10.40pm', a classic 'youth culture' hang-out of the time with its formica tables, jukebox and coffee served in glass cups and saucers. Andrew Koumi, a Greek Cypriot bought it in 1961 and ran it until the summer of 2014 when he retired aged 81.

Catering for students from the nearby College of Further Education (CFE) which opened on Cowley Road in 1949, (full title the Robert Cecil Percy Schools of Technology, Art and Commerce, Principal one John Henry Brookes) workers in the many businesses on Cowley Road, and car workers from the Pressed Steel and Body Plants in Cowley, the menu was the traditional fare of eggs, hamburgers, chips, baked beans and omelettes with tea and coffee, but with a Mediterranean twist. Andrew introduced stuffed peppers and aubergines and moussaka, 'my favourite dish'.

The well-known IT company, Research Machines (RM) was one of those businesses founded and developed over

Andrew Kuomi (inset)
and The Excelsior, 2014.

ANDREW KUOMI'S MOUSSAKA

This version is the one that Andrew Kuomi used in the Excelsior for decades. His is an adaptation of Rick's Stein's recipe and was one of the dishes Andrew served as a 'special'. Serves 6.

900 g lean minced lamb • 3 large aubergines
1 large onion finely chopped • 1 400 g can chopped tomatoes
3 garlic cloves crushed
Handful of fresh oregano leaves (dried is fine)
1 sp ground cinnamon • 175 ml olive oil
50 ml white wine • Salt and freshly ground black pepper

For the topping *75 g butter • 75 g plain flour • 600 ml milk*
50 g parmesan cheese, finely grated
2 medium free-range eggs, beaten

Pre heat the oven to 200°c/gas mark 6. For the lamb sauce, heat two teaspoons of the oil in a pan. Add the onions and garlic and fry till just beginning to brown. Add the minced lamb and fry over a high heat for 3–4 minutes. Add the wine, tomatoes, cinnamon and oregano and simmer gently for 30–40 minutes. While this is cooking slice the stalks off the aubergines and cut them lengthways in to 5 mm slices. Heat the frying pan until really hot, add one tablespoon of the oil and a layer of aubergine slices and fry quickly until tender and lightly coloured on each side. Lift out and layer over the base of a 2.5 litre shallow ovenproof dish and season lightly with salt and pepper. Then add a layer of lamb sauce and repeat with the rest of the aubergines and lamb sauce, seasoning each layer.

For the topping, melt the butter in a non-stick pan. Add the flour and cook over a medium heat for one minute to cook the flour. Gradually beat in the milk, bring to the boil, stirring, and leave to simmer gently for 10 minutes stirring every so often. Stir in the cheese and some salt and pepper. Cool slightly and beat in the eggs. Pour over the topping and bake for 25–30 minutes.

lunches in the Excelsior by Mike Fischer and Mike O'Regan. Their premises were at various locations on Cowley Road in the 1970s. Mike O'Regan says that they ate there every day for almost three years and '*I learned that it was normal to have chips with spaghetti bolognese.*' But the café had a reputation far beyond east Oxford.

Andrew recalls: '*I had a Saudi Prince in here once. His chauffer tried to book a table, but he got the wrong Excelsior. He meant to go to the one at the top of the Woodstock Road, the Excelsior Hotel, but he got directed here!*'

Another customer was the future chef Rick Stein, who became a regular in the late 1960s when he was an undergraduate. More recently restaurant entrepreneur Clinton Pugh acknowledged the Excelsior's influence on his cafés saying that he used to hang out and check out his style, amongst other things, adopting the glass coffee cups *'because that way you can tell the coffee is quality'*.

The Excelsior remained almost unchanged throughout its time, with a clattering till and chuntering pink-and-chrome Gaggia coffee machine, right to the last day. The coffee was always a pleasant surprise. Andrew confided that he always used organic coffee beans which he ground himself in the café, despite their expense, but nonetheless always kept his prices well below those of the trendy coffee chains springing up around him. But they took their toll. He told me that by the end, takings had dropped 50% from their heyday when he employed two chefs and four waitresses in the café. But both the CFE on Cowley Road and most of the Cowley car plant had closed too. As he put it, *'Now I do everything myself . . .it's the competition . . . instead of ten other cafés [on Cowley Road] there are now fifty!'*

The café's image was decidedly gothic. One student guide to Oxford described it in 2000 as *'a strange and frightening world . . . a cross between Twin Peaks and a Mike Leigh film . . . its ambience of mystique provided by a dense cloud of cigarette smoke while piped music has been replaced in favour of the* *sound of hacking coughs . . . If you like an element of surrealism and horror with your eating experiences this is the real McCoy.'*

But it was the loyal locals, many from the margins of society, who appreciated the hospitality and sense of unhurried welcome in the café, who nominated him for the Community Award he won in 2012 that kept it going for so many years.

A TASTE OF ASIA

The small grocery shops were changing too. Immigrants from Pakistan, Bangladesh and to a lesser extent India, began arriving in Oxford from the early 1960s. Raja Bros was the first and best known Asian store. Run by brothers Anwar and Manzoor Raja, it started out on Bullingdon Road before transferring to 228–230 Cowley Road in 1968. Local people considered it to be the hub of the Asian and Caribbean communities for many years, selling Indian, Pakistani and Caribbean foodstuffs. The brothers lived above the shop. Raja Bros copied and was the successor to Eddie's. When they got going Eddie retired. One young man from Bangladesh, Manju Miah who arrived in the summer of 1972 and was still at

Eastern and Continental Stores.

The Moonlight, 1995, and
Manju Miah (below).

school, remembers Cowley Road at the time as a place where
most of the businesses were boarded up.

*'In the early days I was afraid to walk the streets. But Asians
took on the boarded up shops. Asian businesses rescued Cowley
Road.'*

Raja Bros thrived and were joined by Eastern &
Continental Stores who moved from Walton St to the
corner of Crown St in 1978 and are still there, and by Akash
Khan's store at no 214. There were no Afro-Caribbean run
shops. Their fresh food and grocery needs were supplied by
enterprising Asian shopkeepers.

While many Pakistanis worked on the buses, they also
specialised in shops, including newsagents, hardware shops
and clothes shops as well as groceries, while the Bangladeshi
community opened restaurants, 95% of 'Indian' restaurants
are operated by Bangladeshis according to one local.
The Oxford Bangladeshi community, like most British
Bangladeshis, is overwhelmingly from one area, the Sylhet
region of northeast Bangladesh.

MOONLIGHT ON COWLEY ROAD

After the Himalay Restaurant opened in 1962 it was followed by the Kashmir in 1971 and the Anglo-Indian and the Moti Mahal on St Clements.

One of the most successful and enduring was the Moonlight. It started out in 1974 when Manju Miah left school and rented what was effectively a wreck. It had been a small cafeteria, 'the Moonlight' that was almost derelict, had just 18 seats and was the hangout of the east Oxford squatting community. There was hardly a kitchen worth the name – it just had a plastic corrugated wall.

'It was a real struggle at first as I didn't have the experience. I was straight out of school and had only moved from Bangladesh the previous year.'

But he worked 9am to 3am every day. It helped that he lived just round the corner in Circus Street and gradually expanded it, purchasing the lease on no 58 for £3,000 with the support of his uncle Akash Khan. In the early days he was taking £25 per week. By 1978 he was looking to expand and arranged for the premised to be upgraded including a new roof.

'The builder took off the old one and then refused to replace it unless he was paid in full in advance. This was a crisis moment for me. I went to see my bank manager Bill Crouch at the Nat West Cowley Road East branch to ask for a loan. He asked me what security I had. "None sir, except my word". Bill said, "I will come over to the restaurant at 12.30". He had lunch there and when he left he said "Come and see me at 3pm". When I got there he asked me again about security and got the same answer – just my word. He looked at me and said, "I'm near retirement now and I've never taken a real risk. Now I will. Don't let me down." He lent me the money I needed. We never looked back. We repaid the loan in full within a year and bought the freehold a few years later. Bill was crucial and the success of a lot of other local Asian businesses is down to him.'

The Moonlight grew rapidly and expanded from 24 seats to 250, taking over premises on either side to become the second biggest restaurant in Oxford (after Brown's on St Giles). Turnover went from £25 to £30,000 a week. One successful strategy for attracting custom and coverage was support for the student Oxford Majlis Asian Society.

The Hi-Lo Jamaican Eating House.

'We used to sponsor their VIP visitors, providing a free meal for them and the Society's officers after every talk. It really helped spread the word about us.'

Miah sold the business in 1990 but it continued to trade until 2010.

HI-LO: 'FROM A PENNY TO A THOUSAND POUNDS'

Afro Caribbean restaurants were a much rarer phenomenon. Two opened in the early 1980s, The Jamaican Hi-Lo Eating House in 1981 and the Carlton Blue in 1983.

The 'Hi-Lo' has become something of a Cowley Road institution. Andy Anderson and his wife Jan moved from Bristol in 1979 and initially started selling fruit and veg from no 70 before developing the restaurant and expanding into no 68 in 1989. The restaurant rapidly acquired a reputation as an exotic and authentic Jamaican cabin-style place where genuine rastas hung out. Students flocked to it, amongst others Prime Minister David Cameron, who lived across the road at no 69. The oft-told story of Cameron babysitting the children is exaggerated.

'He was a bit of a regular and sometimes when Andy got called to the bar David [Cameron] would sit with Daniel [their

The Carlton Blue, 1995.

baby son] on his lap and do counting games with him. He was a good guy, we liked him, but he never actually babysat.'

The restaurant didn't have a licensed bar at some points and this was resolved by selling small sandwiches for 25p with each drink. Andy did nothing to dispel the rasta image. Another Jamaican trader on Cowley Road admired his skill.

'He was a bit of an actor. He purported to be a real rasta-person but it was a bit of a cloak. He was very intelligent and created an image - extremely successfully.'

The *Inspector Morse* series regularly used Cowley Road as a backdrop and one episode featured the Hi-Lo, though after a

✺ CURRIED GOAT

This is a home version of the Hi-Lo signature dish. Goat meat is very much the culinary 'new kid on the block' these days. Serves 4.

700 g goat shoulder, diced
1 large onion, finely chopped
400 m can red kidney, pinto or black eyed beans
400 g tin chopped tomatoes
10 garlic cloves, crushed
100 g fresh ginger, finely chopped
2 scotch bonnet chillies, chopped (hot)
100 ml sunflower oil
Small handful curry leaves
4 tbsp mild curry powder
sm bunch of coriander, chopped
3 sprigs thyme
½ lemon, juiced
350 ml beef stock
2 tsp salt

Heat the oil in a large casserole dish.

Mix in the onion, garlic and ginger and cook until softened. Add chillies, curry leaves, thyme, curry powder and salt. Cook for 2–3 minutes.

Tip the diced goat into the pan.

Cook for five minutes over a medium high heat until the meat has browned. Add chopped tomatoes and stock. Increase the heat, bring to the boil for 10 minutes.

Reduce the heat, cover and leave to simmer gently for two hours. Remove the lid for the final 30 minutes. Check occasionally to see there is enough liquid.

Add the beans and top up with chilli if you like it spicy.

After five minutes, remove from the heat. Add the lemon juice and coriander and stir well.

Serve with warmed roti and rice.

Valerie Ricketts, proprietor of Ricks.

disagreement about the fee most of it ended up being shot in a city hotel.

Part of the image was the Hi-Lo's informality, which apparently extended to its pricing policy, proclaimed on the front of the restaurant 'from a penny to a thousand pounds' with the customers being charged what Andy thought they could afford. Student guides advised dressing down to avoid being overcharged, but there wasn't any truth in it. Jan explained the reality,

'We had a spoken menu, nothing was written down, but the prices were fixed and in the early days you could have a monkey nut for just 1p.'

These days a printed menu is displayed in the window and the prices remain remarkably cheap, starters at £2.50–£3 and main courses for £8.50–£9.50 with vegetarian options at £8. *'We don't really do desserts,'* Jan added, *'the servings are so huge everybody is full before then'.*

Top selling dishes are jerk chicken and curried goat. Most of the goat is bought from Eastern and Continental Stores up the road and Hi-Lo have always had a commitment to buy from other local traders including Alder's, Tahmid Stores and Meli.

The only other Afro Caribbean restaurant to make an impression on Cowley Road was 'Ricks'. Opened in 1987 by Valerie Ricketts and two of her sons.

It was a 'proper restaurant, not a cookhouse'. Some members of the Afro-Caribbean community found the presence of the Hi-Lo embarrassing. Initially it thrived, serving just Caribbean dishes and attracting a student crowd, but didn't get the support of the local community and went bankrupt five years later. Meanwhile thirty years after it opened, the Hi-Lo is still in business and still trading on its authentic 'Jamaican cabin' atmosphere.

THE 'IRON CURTAIN' OPENS

While Eddie's deli may have been run by a Polish refugee, Polish and Eastern European foods were not prominent on Cowley Road until some years after the fall of the Iron Curtain. The charmingly named Russian Fairytale supermarket opened in 1997. Run by a Ukranian called Raissa Goutsal, she was delighted when Oxford twinned with the Russian city of Perm. Perm was a 'closed city' until 1991 and reputedly was the centre of bicycle manufacture for the USSR. This seems to have been a front for rockets and missiles.

Raissa's specialities were borscht, the Russian staple pelmeni, and of course vodka.

Russian Fairytale's range of foodstuffs attracted a clientele from right across the eastern European community as well as Oxford's Russian community of about 800, mainly students and academics, as well as adventurous Brits. But Raissa moved over into the travel business and the shop was taken over and rebranded Baltic Foods, run by another Ukranian, Ludmilla Berenis. Now it is less a travel agency and more a place for the imagination to wander while smelling the aroma of Lithuanian bread, Polish sausages, 'herring underneath the coat' (raw herrings in layers with potato, carrot and beetroot), gherkins, mushrooms, cabbage and sour cream. Her near neighbour 'Hajduczek' was the first Polish restaurant on Cowley Road, opening in 2001 and has been followed by a plethora of Polish shops – run by Iranians, Bangladeshis (as was Hajduczek) or indeed anyone who wasn't Polish.

Kazbar, the best tapas bar in the country.

COWLEY'S 'MASH UP'

This 'mash up' trend began around 2001 when Hajduczek, opened. Paying a visit with Asian friends I was surprised to find the menu being discussed in Bangla, as the front of house staff were all Bangladeshi. Enquiring how this could be in a Polish restaurant I was told,

'There are far too many Indian restaurants on Cowley Road, so we thought we would diversify. But we have a Polish chef.'

The menu reflected its exotic origins including such well known 'Polish' items as basmati rice and mango. More authentically it claimed to sell 100 different varieties of vodka.

✹ PERM PELMENI

I first came across pelmeni on various trips to Oxford's twin city Perm in the Urals in the 1990s. Pelmeni, or pierogi, as it is known in Poland and eastern Europe, is not unlike ravioli or Chinese wonton.

In Perm they are often made with mushrooms or vegetables such as turnips and onions. However their real purpose was as a way of storing food throughout the Siberian winter. Pelmeni were made in their hundreds or even thousands, using cows and pigs slaughtered to avoid feeding them through the winter and then stored outside in the Arctic conditions. Superior versions were made with reindeer or even bear meat.

Rather than make your own I recommend you go and buy them. Ask for pierogi in Polish shops. Cook them like ravioli. They are cooked when they float to the top.

Cook from frozen, even if you make them yourself- freeze them for at least 24 hours after you have made them. A 50/50 mix of beef and pork is the traditional filling.

Serve them with sour cream and a rough, chopped tomato and cucumber salad. If you want to keep it plain, stick to sour cream and chopped dill plus salt and pepper. Accompany with vodka.

Café CoCo.

Majid Chatar outside Maroc Deli.

One of them said to me: *'Let's face it, fusion is where it's at now. Chicken Tikka Masala is a Scottish dish!'*

Restaurant entrepreneur Clinton Pugh also likes the multi-cultural nature of Cowley Road's food scene and sees the emerging fusion trend as a real positive: *'I have a feeling that a café could be anywhere. To flourish it needs to be classic, timeless with a contemporary and creative twist. Ethnic cafés as such don't help in the long term. Diversity yes, but with an artistic and creative content'.*

This is the 'modern British' approach, as expressed on Cowley Road. The food is pizza, pasta and other loosely Mediterranean-inspired dishes such as the 'breakfast pizza' and 'super food salads with salmon' – *'our best seller,'* says Pugh, combined with the almost ubiquitous pulled pork.

Pugh has had a huge impact on Cowley Road since he opened his first restaurant, Café Coco, in April 1992 'in peak recession'. A designer by profession, he started out turning round restaurants such as Clarrie's on Little Clarendon Street. It is Cowley Road where the Pugh empire has become established, but along the way it has included amongst others, the Grand Café on the High Street and the Lemon

Tree in Summertown. Apart from Coco, Clint has opened cafés up and down Cowley Road including Café Baba, The Organic Burger Bar, Kasbar and Café Tarifa. All of them are design-led and aimed at a better off clientele who care about the atmosphere.

They didn't all work, particularly the Organic Burger Bar; *'Everyone assumed it was expensive because it had the word organic in the title'* and Café Baba struggled because there was 'nowhere to park' and was sold in 2007. But generally the combination of decor and food has been a success. Kasbar has been called the best tapas bar in the country. Travel writer, James Attlee evokes the Kasbar atmosphere:

'designed to evoke a North African souk with yellow walls and Islamic inspired metal grilles in the windows. Inside the walls are decorated with turquoise and aquamarine tiles. On summer evenings a retractable roof is rolled back so that one can dine beneath the sky accompanied by the screams of swifts as they swoop for insects.'

Atlee characterises it as 'an idealised but nonetheless enjoyable fiction' before contrasting it with the real thing across the road, the North African, Maroc Deli. Oxford rock band Supergrass called their 1995 first album *I Should Coco*, allegedly after their time spent in the café. The album went on to sell over a million copies worldwide and gained platinum status.

Maroc Deli has engaged in no small amount of enjoyable myth-making of its own, its proprietor Majid Chatar proudly telling me that it has had three visits from BBC TV and even one from Moroccan TV. The various varieties of *merguez*, Moroccan sausage, all made on the premises at the back are a particular draw, but the rest of the shop is itself a kaleidoscope of the changing food tastes of Cowley Road shoppers.

Another modern British entrepreneur, Drew Brammer has also made his mark locally. Although he also owns Cowley Road-based coffee shop Keen Bean, his focus has been slightly wider, founding and then selling on the popular and trendy Oxfork and in 2015 opening The Chester Arms off Iffley Road as a gastro pub. Oxfork has

❦ MERGUEZ PAELLA

Traditionally paella has involved a mixture of fish, shellfish, chicken and chorizo sausage. This recipe takes account of location. Shellfish aren't readily available on Cowley Road, Oxford being about as far away from the sea as you can get in England. There are plenty of different paella recipes and most of them involve a mixture of chicken, chorizo and seafood so the proportions can vary. You can see the *merguez* sausage (lamb), being made in the back of Maroc Deli. Serves 4.

150 g merguez sausage chopped up small • 50 g chicken breasts or thighs cut into small pieces • 4 slices bacon cut into pieces • 10 king prawns or a larger number of frozen prawns • 250 g fresh fish such as haddock or a similar quantity of dried fish • 300 g arborio rice or paella rice, such as bomba • 1 large onion • 3 cloves of garlic 150 g fresh or frozen peas, broad beans or green beans (chopped up) • 2 large ripe tomatoes, chopped or 1 red pepper, sliced • 600 ml vegetable or chicken stock 4 tbsp olive oil • 1 tsp turmeric or a pinch of saffron A few sprigs of fresh thyme • A couple of sprigs of flat leaf parsley • 1 lemon • A glass of white wine

Heat the oil in a pan and add the onion and the garlic, crushed. Make sure to soften, not burn. Add the sliced merguez and the bacon and fry until browned and crispy. Boil the water and stir in the stock to a simmer and add the saffron/turmeric. Pour in the wine and lemon juice too. Cook the haddock in a little water for five minutes and leave to cool. Remove the flesh from the skin and flake. Add the rice to the pan with the onion and garlic, chop the thyme and add the bacon, chicken and merguez sausage too. Pour in a cup of the hot stock and stir well to stop the rice from sticking. Keep an eye on the mixture and when the stock is absorbed, add the rest gradually. When the rice is nearly cooked add the tomatoes/peppers, the peas/beans and the haddock and stir in. Cover the pan with tin foil and place in a preheated oven 180˚c/gas mark 4 for 10–12 minutes. Remove, add some coarsely chopped flat leaf parsley as garnish and serve with lemon wedges.

entrenched Magdalen Road as a new food destination along with neighbours Oli's Thai, The Rusty Bicycle, The Madgalen Arms and the long established Magic Café. The unusual mix of residential and commercial, so much more common in east Oxford 70 years ago, has endured on Magdalen Road, with new arrivals like the upmarket wholefood shop Wild Honey joining established traders like Noor Halal.

FUSION FORTUNES

The trend towards 'fusion' of the 'Indian/Thai/Chinese/ Continental' variety such as First Floor is now well established, and specialist outlets like 'dessert parlours' such as Temptations and Sundaes Gelato thrive as a non-alcoholic alternative to the pub culture.

The high point for Indian restaurants on Cowley Road was about 2002. Annie Skinner reports nine in 2004. With the closure of a Cowley Road institution, Mirch Masala, in early 2015, there are now only five left, and many of these have followed the trend morphing into Nepalese or Nepalese/Indian since about 2009, when the Everest opened in Howard Street, quickly followed by Yeti and Kadai & Naan, whose menu charmingly includes Chicken Cowley '. . . *Cowley Road's own local dish*' under the Chef's Nepalese specials. The food is essentially the same i.e. north Indian – with added dumplings, 'momo', but the market has changed as traditional Indian food has gradually fallen out of fashion.

The economic viability of Indian restaurants has become more problematic too. Quite a few restaurants relied on a pool of casual labour paid in cash, whether it be students taking on shifts between studying or on graduation, or unskilled workers from Bangladesh joining their families for short periods. Immigration rules have changed and tightened up. The pool has shrunk and restaurant owners now find themselves paying formerly unheard of overheads like PAYE and the minimum wage, to keep staff. As Oxford property prices, both residential and commercial, have risen, there has been a trend toward shifting operations to less expensive locations in the suburbs like Temple Cowley

Aziz Rahman (inset) owner of the Aziz Restaurant.

and Rose Hill, and to outlying villages such as Kidlington, Wheatley and Kennington.

AZIZ ARRIVES

The early Asian shops began to change too. Shops like Raja Bros changed hands. The brothers wanted to retire and successfully applied for planning permission to change the shop's use to a restaurant. It became Aziz Restaurant and opened in 1990. Aziz Rahman, started out as a waiter. Looking to set up his own place, he walked into several restaurants on the street and cheekily asked if they were for sale *'I was shown the door by a very angry Joe at La Capannina'*, but on trying the same trick at Bunter's Bistro, he struck lucky and he and three partners were in possession within six weeks. It became the Star of Asia, but Aziz hankered after something bigger and better.

His enthusiasm for the trade was picked up by reviewers and in an interview with the *Oxford Mail's* Jim O'Callaghan, on being asked where all his passion and enthusiasm came from said: *'I feel like the host of a party every night – and the beauty of it is that I get paid for it. I make every effort to make people go out feeling happy'.*

Over the years this restaurant has become one of the best known in Oxford and as its success grew Aziz opened a chain of eponymous restaurants across Oxfordshire and the Cotswolds. The tone and style are consciously upmarket and Aziz has made great efforts, not least through his membership of the Ethnic Minority Business Service and the sponsorship of events ranging from Cowley Road Carnival to the Nowka Bais (Bangladeshi regatta) to raise the dining profile of Cowley Road.

'The early days were very exciting,' recalls Aziz. 'Me and Clint [Pugh], transformed Cowley Road in terms of cuisine. We wanted people staying in places like the Randolph and the Old Parsonage Hotel to come to Cowley Road to eat. It has worked, but I'm afraid Headington and Summertown are still smarter.'

Aziz is, in his own way, the epitome of the modern British restaurateur.

❉ MACH BHAJA BANGLADESH FISH AZIZ-STYLE

Bangladesh is renowned for its fish cuisine. So it is no surprise that many Bangladeshi fish recipes have transferred with them to east Oxford. There is a long tradition of serving high quality Bangladeshi food on Cowley Road and a number of the shops have a wide range of dried and frozen fish imported from South Asia.

This is a home version of something Aziz Rahman and I have eaten in his restaurant after meetings of the Ethnic Minority Business Service. So it has good memories and Aziz still serves it. Serves 3–4.

6 steak pieces of king fish or hilsa
2–3 green chillies, deseeded and finely chopped
1 tsp turmeric
1 tsp garam masala
1 lime, juiced
2–3 garlic cloves, crushed
4 tbsp sunflower oil

For garnish
1 red onion, chopped
1 lemon, sliced into wedges

Marinade the fish steaks in the garlic, spices and lime juice for four hours.

Heat a pan with the oil and shallow fry the fish steaks on a medium-low heat until slightly charred, turning gently.

Serve with chopped raw red onion and lemon wedges, dal and steamed rice.

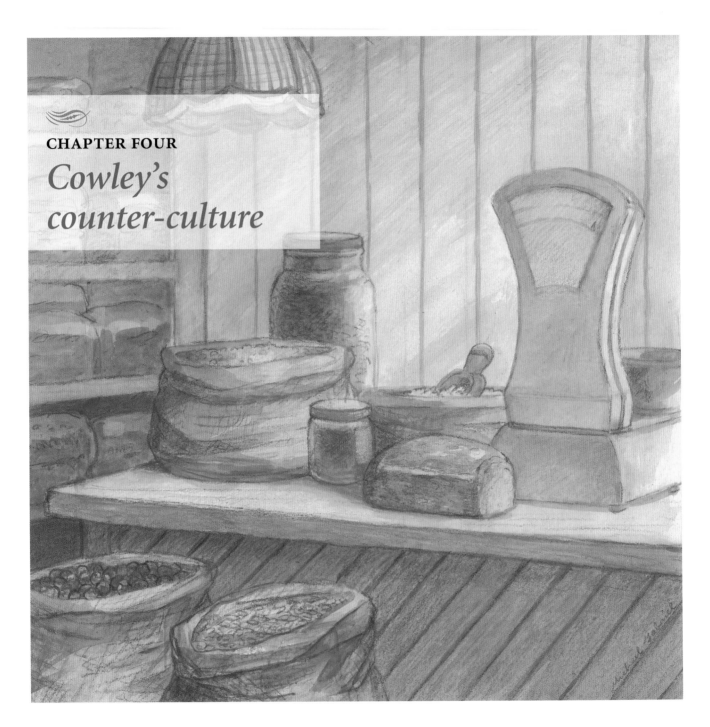

CHAPTER FOUR
Cowley's counter-culture

Although Ancient Greek philosopher Pythagoras advocated vegetarianism, known then as the Pythagorean Diet (yes there really is nothing new under the sun) vegetarianism was essentially an approach to food based on religious belief and ritual, such as the forswearing of meat during Lent, or the Hindu tradition of vegetarianism in India. It was more a matter of necessity for poor people until the 18th century. It was only during that century that vegetarianism – based on ethical conviction and the radical ideas associated with the agrarian communists called the Diggers and the republican Levellers of the English Revolution – could be said to come into existence. The first identifiable vegetarian cookbook, *Primitive Cookery, or the Kitchen Garden Displayed* was published in 1767.

Unsurprisingly such an eclectic place as Oxford has its radical traditions in food as much as in other dimensions of politics. The poet Shelley, an undergraduate at University College at the turn of the 19th century, was an early and vociferous advocate of vegetarianism. He was expelled in 1811 after he published a tract *The necessity of atheism* and for his admiration of the revolutionary Thomas Paine.

Although the Vegetarian Society was founded in 1847, throughout the 19th century vegetarianism was considered extremely odd. A Mrs Brotherton published a cookbook in 1821 entitled, *A New System of Vegetable Cookery* and this was followed in 1847 by the anonymous *A Few Recipes of Vegetarian Diet*, but it was thin pickings.

However, Oxford, being the home of lost causes, by no mean rejected vegetarianism and as long ago as 1908, my copy of *Alden's Guide* includes an advertisement for the 'Japanese café' on the High Street featuring its 'special menu for vegetarians'. In fact vegetarian restaurants were relatively popular from the end of the 19th century. They offered value for money and were patronised by people who found a vegetarian meal pleasantly different as long as they didn't have to eat it all the time. This more tolerant approach reflected a gradual change in the national diet towards more fruit and vegetables, more milk consumption and the increased availability of chilled fruit imported from Australia and New Zealand. It was also a response to the shock of the discovery

Uhuru shop, 2015.

of just how poor the health of the nation was due to poor nutritional standards, when attempts to recruit fit and healthy young men to fight the Boer War (1899–1902) proved so difficult.

One key figure in this nutritional revolution at the time was a Swiss doctor, Maximillian Bircher-Benner who in 1895 after suffering from jaundice himself became an advocate of raw foods as a way to health. As well as experimenting successfully, with raw fruit and vegetables, it was his invention of muesli that made his name. Allegedly discovered during a long walk in the mountains with a shepherd, it consisted of coarsely ground wheat soaked in milk sweetened with honey, eaten with an apple. He began to serve it for breakfast at his clinic and the rest is history.

UHURU AND THE WHOLEFOOD REVOLUTION

As Cowley Road began to revive in the early 1970s after the ravages of the planning blight of the previous three decades, it is not surprising that it began to attract the attention of the radical end of the student community and with it that strand involved in food politics – the spiritual descendants of Shelley. The first expression of this was the establishment of Uhuru in 1974. Uhuru meaning 'freedom' in Swahili has a unique, almost mythical place in the history of the wholefood movement and as part of the scenery of Cowley Road. It began life as a café, which sold wholefoods and handicrafts from collectives in Africa in a shop across the road. It acted as a focus for campaigning on a range of issues from third world liberation and development to community politics and mental health issues.

Its origins were in the student-based group Third World First, itself located on Cowley Road and now People and Planet, a national student campaigning organisation which is still headquartered in east Oxford. Student agitation around trade deals with former colonial nations such as sugar-producing Caribbean islands, fundraising for famine relief in Ethiopia and the like, led to discussions about a local centre to promote campaigns around development and to engage actively, by importing and selling items from developing countries, particularly those produced by co-operatives. These were idealistic days and there was a focus on the Tanzanian socialism of Julius Nyrere and the Ujamaa village model. This was in retrospect, the 'phase one' Uhuru. Annie Skinner quotes one of the founders:

'When it was started, Uhuru was run by fairly conventional left/liberals who wore shoes and fairly clean clothes and ate meat. A silversmith set up his smithy in the store and someone else started a shelf of whole foods. Before long the Third World handicrafts had been shoved inexorably into one half of the shop while the whole foods expanded. Trucks were delivering 100 lb bags of brown rice and 120 lb bags of hazelnuts, large quantities of oats, raisins and other dried fruit . . .'.

Uhuru had a core of paid workers, the founder members and a host of volunteers who together operated as a collective. Skinner quotes one member who recalls the atmosphere as one where community action, the politics of food and a collective approach to management were simply assumed:

'We were radically egalitarian – going for consensus at our meetings – an equal voice for everyone. People joined the collective easily – I don't recall what membership rules we had. The group grew. Soon there were eleven people living above the store. Some were very much into the wholefoods, vegetarian cooking and holistic health. . . . Soon meat was banished from the kitchen upstairs and it was never even contemplated for the café.'

Uhuru shop (left), and Uhuru Café, 1981.

One young volunteer, Hafiz Ladell who went on to found The Magic Café, was an undergraduate at Oxford University at the time and summarised the zeitgeist:

'. . . the revolution was very much about the sort of food you ate and the way you ate it. It didn't take me long to identify myself as a vegetarian: not only was it an act of solidarity with the wretched of the earth but it was a way of forcing a double-take in all sorts of social situations in which consensus participation was expected. Being vegetarian in those days required either an infinite tolerance of indifferent omelette or else demanded a bold exploration of the exciting possibilities of brown rice and soya beans, largely uncharted territory at the time . . . . Just over Magdalen Bridge on the threshold of Alternative Oxford that was Cowley Road, Uhuru Café was a haven for like-minded souls. Barefoot cooking, customer washing up, "end of the world" stew, the bizarre rituals of bourgeois dining were turned upside down.'

MUESLI MOVEMENT

Another volunteer recalls an epic trip with her boyfriend. Just graduated from Cambridge, they toured England on a tandem in the summer of 1977, visiting communes and alternative initiatives, WWOOF-ing (Working Weekends on Organic Farms) up and down the land, ending up at Uhuru. Already its fame had spread. She was interested in co-ops and collectives, growing organic food and community action/alternative communities. It ticked all the boxes. They volunteered.

'It was a community and political information hub which sold wholefoods, at the front. The back was where the stuff was stored, bagged etc. There was a huge vat for mixing the muesli.

It was all very exotic, very exciting and political. I barely knew what muesli was when I arrived. We were expected to take turns in the Café kitchen too. You would arrive in the morning and your job was to prep and cook for an unknown number of customers – soups, stews, flapjacks, crumbles – all cooked from scratch by people some of whom hardly knew how to cook, let alone for large numbers. We had our disasters. One day a huge box of plums arrived from a well wisher in the Vale of Evesham. We decided to make jam. We poured the jam into giant glass sweet jars placed on the stone floor. Within 30 seconds of the jam

✄ END OF THE WORLD STEW

The 'Uhuru Cooking Guide' from which this recipe is taken, may be only 40 years old, but the terms it uses feel, in some cases, more exotic today than those in many 16th century cookbooks. There is a section on the cooking of 'Red Wonder Beans', which research seems to suggest, must have been organic red kidney beans imported from Tanzania. This is an updated version which tries to stick to the spirit of the original recipe. The recipe is described as being 'for many people'; I estimate serves about 8.

350 g 'red wonder beans', aka, red kidney beans, organic or not, pre-soaked for 12 hours
3 large onions, chopped
500 g carrots, sliced • 250 g parsnips, diced
500 green cabbage, thinly sliced
3 large tomatoes, sliced, or one tin of chopped tomatoes
1 tbsp miso • 1 tsp salt • A few basil leaves

Mix all the ingredients together in a large saucepan and add 1½ litres of water. Bring to the boil, cover and simmer for one hour. Serve in bowls with tamari (Japanese non-wheat soy-like sauce), a jacket potato and butter.

filling the jars they cracked and hot jam and glass shards flowed all over the floor, under the doors, into the café and under the kitchen cupboards. It took weeks to clear up.'

The collective soon realised that it wasn't just them who didn't know how to cook wholefoods. Not many of their customers did either, which restricted sales. That winter the collective sat down and wrote *The Uhuru Cooking Guide*.

In the spirit of the times the book has no 'author'. The introduction explains its purpose:

'... many people have asked how to cook the various grains, pulses, flours and other oddities sold in Uhuru. On the café side we try to present these foods in a simple way but it is not always possible for the cook of the day to explain how and why he or she has cooked such a meal. So eventually we have produced a short cooking guide that may answer some of the questions and will hopefully stimulate you to experiment with recipes of your own making.'

The book is organised around explaining how to cook basic whole foods, brown rice, lentils, soya beans, split peas or what they refer to as 'red wonder beans', with a couple of recipes for each; dishes with names like 'winter stew' or 'lentil pie'.

Prominent amongst the recipes, in the 'cereal flakes' section is the Uhuru muesli recipe. Muesli was the iconic food of this revolutionary and 'alternative' world.

Such was the status of this new food in 'alternative' circles that the east Oxford/Cowley Road area soon acquired the partly affectionate, partly derisive nickname, 'the muesli belt'.

These were also the early days of Fair Trade, though the term hadn't been invented yet. Uhuru took the initiative and established 'Campaign Coffee', fair-trade instant coffee imported from co-operatives in Tanzania. In 1977 two and a half tonnes was imported for sale in the shop. A volunteer recalls the result:

'It was a fine dried powder in silver foil packages. Somewhere during transit many of the packages were damaged and moisture got in, turning them instantly into coffee 'bricks'. We couldn't sell them. All the time I was there we used to hack lumps off these unsaleable bricks in the back to make coffee for the volunteers. The taste was fairly terrible and it was a financial disaster, but it was a brave thing to do.'

The atmosphere was heady, even revolutionary. The collective members were heavily involved in a range of local initiatives including an adventure playground, welfare rights, housing action and a women's refuge. The café hosted the entire gamut of political campaigns and causes including abortion rights, anti-nuclear and peace groups, gay groups, anti-fascist groups, the Claimants Union, liberation and

Annette Mngxitama; Uhuru's longest serving member.

Uhuru shop; mixing the muesli and playing loud reggae music.

human rights groups. Several city-wide projects had their inaugural meetings in Uhuru including the 'Free University of Cowley' in 1976. One worker during this period describes the mixture of revolutionary fervour and pragmatism:

'We were one of the first workers' collectives in this country; there were a few others . . . Suma . . . we bought our goods from them, which all came in sacks. . . we packed them in bags with political statements on them so we were linked with all the other collectives and then we wrote a book on running a collective ['Uhuru: A Working Alternative'*] which was not a best seller but you know, we were pleased with it . . . [Uhuru] was very functional . . . we worked very well . . . and it was very exciting. For example although I worked in the café, when we were running short of bags of food in the shop I instigated reggae nights where we would all go and play loud reggae music and*

✳ THE ORIGINAL UHURU MUESLI

Anyone connected with Cowley Road will at one time or another have heard the area being referred to as the 'muesli belt'. It is a reference both to its bohemian and counter-cultural origins, the presence of the whole foods available in the area long before they were anywhere else and its greenish-tinged contemporary image. Despite all this baggage, it is a great breakfast cereal and very versatile. It is also a great snack, not just at breakfast.

This recipe borrows from the original Uhuru recipe devised in the mid 1970s and is a more robust version than the glorified 'oats with a bit of fruit and a toasted nut'-type recipes often found in cook books these days. It harks back to the original version developed by Dr Bircher-Benner

To create the base, mix together:
200 g small oats
75 g jumbo oats
75 g wheat flakes
75 g barley flakes
75 g rye flakes
120 g mixed dried fruit (sultanas, currants, raisins and dates)
75 g chopped mixed nuts (almonds, walnuts and hazel nuts are good)

One handful of muesli is enough for a single helping. Soaking overnight in apple juice or milk improves the muesli. Add whatever fresh or cooked seasonal fruit is available e.g. apple, banana, pear, plum, rhubarb or soft fruit like raspberries or loganberries.

Serve with milk, yoghurt and a little honey to taste.

pack until about one in the morning and have the greatest time. I can declare it now because it's so many years later, I think health and safety was different then. I think it was at one of those sessions that my son's hamster disappeared!'

Such episodes and issues like being unable to shut the oven door without placing a fire extinguisher against it, meant that even in this freewheeling atmosphere, health and safety loomed large. The café was forced to shut for a year in 1979-80 while 'the community' rebuilt the kitchen and installed a second toilet. By the time the café was ready to reopen, the Uhuru Collective had undergone a transformation. A second phase had begun.

Hafiz, who started to volunteer as a cook in the Uhuru Café when it reopened in 1980 after the refit, takes up the story:

'Barefoot hippy was out, radical feminism had taken over. In accordance with these shifting polarities, graffiti on nearby walls angrily proclaimed "Burn men!". I was having great fun doing volunteer cooking shifts, enjoying the freedom of the café kitchen experimenting with different combinations of ingredients. But it was all on sufferance. Easy-going anarchy was a thing of the past.

One day I came in to discover that the new segregated toilet bore a new sign "Men and other worldwide diseases". This didn't feel at all right to me. Next day I came in equipped with paint and brush and painted the offending words out. It was, as I was well aware at the time, a provocative but necessary action. The response from the Collective was furious and unrestrained . . . I became identified as the arch-patriarch, banned from Uhuru for ever.'

The new collective started by banning men from the kitchen and then extended this, first to the café and then for a few months, until the rather obvious contradictions of forcing women to do all the shopping were pointed out to them, to the shop.

Hafiz recalls what happened next,

'Unsurprisingly having alienated most of its customer base, Uhuru's café very rapidly went under... the collective continued to run the shop, but all the care and hard work that had gone into the kitchen refit seemed to have been in vain. A plan was hatched to form a new collective of women and men working together under the name "Wholemeal" who would lease the kitchen and café

Fairtrade vs. Nescafé on Cowley Road.

from Uhuru. I allowed myself to be persuaded to do some cooking shifts on their behalf. I really loved the idea of a community café. Once again the response was rapid and merciless. An ultimatum was set, either "Wholemeal" cease all connection with me or the lease would be withdrawn. "Wholemeal" refused to be dictated to and the game was indeed over.'

'Wholemeal' never saw the light of day and the café shut for ever. Eventually the café space was taken over by Oxford City Council as a Women's Centre in 1986. It didn't thrive, as too many women felt intimidated by its recent past history. The Council had a wasting asset on its hands and agreed to a property swap, whereby the collective which owned the café building which they didn't use, exchanged it for the shop building which they used but rented from the City Council. The Council then restored and converted the former café building into accommodation for single people.

By this time the political context had changed dramatically, with the election of the Thatcher Government in 1979, the Greenham Common Women's Peace Camp of the early 1980s and the Miners' Strike and its defeat in 1984-85. The nature of Cowley Road and the wholefood revolution set in train by Uhuru and others was shifting and Uhuru's third phase began. Personal politics was becoming more important; at the same time food awareness and the politics of food were becoming more widespread. Other outlets responded to the demand that this generated. A collective member recalls,

'I remember the day when someone came in and announced that Tesco were stocking lentils. Before that we were the only place in town that stocked wholefoods.'

Others were blunter: *'When Tesco started selling muesli, the game was up for whole food shops.'* Uhuru was facing serious competition and not just from Tesco. Asian shops which first appeared on Cowley Road in 1968 also sold lentils, chickpeas, sesame seeds, various beans and flours and other whole foods – and they sold them in bulk and cheaply. The wholefood revolution had gone global.

Uhuru itself still survives as a family-run business over 40 years after it first opened, but now describes itself as a deli-style 'organic health food shop, specialising in organic and fairtrade products' with a wholefood section.

✻ FAIRTRADE CHOCOLATE TRUFFLES

My daughter Alice, taught me this recipe. This will make about 40–50 truffles.

250 ml double cream
300 g Fairtrade bitter chocolate, finely chopped

For the coating:
250 g Fairtrade bitter chocolate, broken
125 g Fairtrade cocoa powder, sifted

You will need several baking trays lined with non-stick parchment paper and optionally, a pastry bag fitted with a ½ inch plain tip. Put the cream into a saucepan and gently heat until boiling. Remove from the heat and let cool for several minutes. Put the chopped chocolate into a heatproof bowl and pour over the hot cream. Set aside for several minutes. Then stir gently until just smooth. Let cool and do not over mix at this stage. When the mixture is cool but not set, beat vigorously with a wooden spoon until thick and much lighter in colour and texture. Using a teaspoon and your hands roll the mixture into balls and place on the baking trays, or spoon the mixture into the pastry bag and pipe the balls onto the trays. Chill until very firm. Put the broken chocolate into a dry heatproof bowl and over a saucepan of steaming, not boiling water, making sure that the water doesn't touch the base of the bowl, or start to boil. Once the chocolate is melted remove the bowl from the heat. Take the chilled balls and, using a couple of forks to balance them on, briefly dip each into the chocolate until coated. Return the coated truffles to the lined trays and leave until the coating is almost set. Roll the truffles in the cocoa powder. Place in the fridge until ready to serve.

Cultivate's organic food Veg Van.

Wholefoods remain an important part of the Cowley Road food scene with Tesco, Sainsbury's, the Co-op and all the Asian shops stocking them. Some, like Tahmid Stores – right across the road from Uhuru and an Aladdin's cave of obscure Indian spices – sell in bulk, partly to the catering trade. The range on offer and the prices charged, are wide, with some items in the supermarkets marketed as 'wholefoods' debatably justifying the name.

By contrast, the People's Supermarket which was established in 2012, positioned itself as an alternative to Tesco, aimed for lower prices. It was correct in identifying the high profit margins on premium organic products sold in supermarkets and attempted to sell them more cheaply. But it soon discovered that most of its customers wanted a wide range of cheap food, organic or not and it went under in little more than a year. It is now a Polish supermarket. Its demise is a reflection perhaps that as with much else in society, the gap between rich and poor is widening and those divisions are expressed in the food we buy and where we buy it.

FROM WHOLE FOOD TO SLOW FOOD: FAIRTRADE, ORGANIC, SEASONAL, LOCAL

Food politics has shifted and reinvented itself over time. Fair trade, organic, seasonal and local is where it is at now. Radical yes, but not revolutionary in the way it was in the mid 1970s.

The Fairtrade movement which had its origins in individual campaigns like the Uhuru 'Campaign Coffee' initiative in the early 1980s has attempted to bridge these gaps by concentrating on products that can be sold at competitive prices and are stocked by mainstream supermarkets. The Fairtrade Foundation was established in 1994 and Oxford City Council declared Oxford a 'Fairtrade City' in 2004. The range of fair-traded produce available has expanded gradually from wine and bananas; Sainsbury's and the Co-op now only stock fair-trade bananas, to encompass sugar, teas, coffees, chocolate, oils, rice and nuts as well as non-food items such as cotton and wool.

In Oxford only the School Ethical Supplies Initiative (SESI) stocks the complete range, and even for them Fairtrade products account for no more that 15% of their turnover. The proportion is less in Uhuru and much less, as percentage of stock, in the supermarkets.

ORGANIC FOOD

Organic food is hardly new. The Soil Association was founded in 1946 and the Henry Doubleday Research Association, now Garden Organic, in 1954. Fruit and vegetables grown in kitchen gardens, on allotments and before that on farms and smallholdings have been largely organic for generations. Demand has been there and early pioneers such as WWOOF have supported the connections between farmers and consumers. Nowadays it is big business with most supermarkets stocking a range of organic fruit and veg and commercial 'veg box' schemes such as Abel & Cole and Riverford having a significant presence. One can hardly turn on the TV for programmes on cooking with organic ingredients or growing organically.

Locally, Cultivate, a co-op established in 2012 to promote the growth and consumption of local, seasonal organic food in Oxford, operate a 'veg van' weekly on Magdalen Road, (by the Rusty Bicycle pub) where they sell their and other local producers organic fruit and vegetables straight to the public. Since 2014 they have been operating a 'click and deliver' on-line veg box scheme as well.

FARMERS' MARKETS

More established are the farmers' market suppliers. The farmers' market idea came over from the USA with the first one in the UK opening in Bath in 1997. East Oxford Farmers' Market began in 2006 supported with a £1,000 grant from local Green Party councillors. Initially based in the Asian Cultural Centre on Manzil Way, it opened each Saturday morning and started with seven stalls and a 'market manifesto' that all the produce had to come from within 30 miles of Oxford. The market proved a huge success and soon outgrew the space, moving to the East Oxford Primary School main hall and playground in early 2009. By 2011 it was a finalist in the BBC 'Food and Farming Awards' as 'Best Food Market' and had a turnover of over £200,000, including

East Oxford Farmers' Market.

a popular pop-up café in one of the classrooms. The core stalls include local farmers, Sandy Lane from Tiddington and Clay's from Warborough, supplying a wide range of their fruit and vegetables as well as, controversially to some, others bought in from further afield and abroad. North Aston and Willowbrook Farms also supply meat, eggs, milk and cream, and various specialist outlets sell local bread, fish, cheese, and in season, juice, soft fruit and nuts.

The location has encouraged a plethora of ethnic stalls too, including South Asian/Indian, Japanese, Tibetan, Greek, Algerian, Moroccan, Filipino and Italian. The clientele is mainly very local with a typical market on a Saturday morning attracting about 700 customers.

GROWING COMMUNITIES, HEALING MINDS

Therapeutic growing was common from the late 19th century. Oxford's Warneford Hospital acquired 13 acres of land in 1876 to become a market garden and this was expanded in the early 20th century when more land was purchased and Warneford Hospital Farm established. In addition to the flowers, fruit and vegetables of the market garden, pigs, poultry and cereal crops were added, as well as an accredited dairy herd. Small groups of patients, accompanied by staff,

worked both the farm and market gardens, including hay making, harvesting crops and caring for the animals. Minutes from the hospital farm sub-committee in September 1944 state that *'The farm should be used for rehabilitation of patients as part of farm policy.'* While most mental hospitals in the country had their hospital farms supplying food for the kitchens and work for the patients, the Ministry of Health shut them down in the years following the establishment of the NHS, with both the farms at Littlemore and Warneford Hospitals closing in the early 1960s. The Warneford farm itself survived until about 1974 with outside contractors managing a dairy herd and selling milk from Cheney farm.

ELDER STUBBS

In the past 30 years the focus has shifted to allotment sites with projects to support vulnerable groups such as that between the Elder Stubbs allotments charity and the mental health charity Restore, which has cultivated a two acre part of the Elder Stubbs site since the late 1980s as part of their therapeutic healing programme. Restore were themselves evicted from land at the Littlemore Hospital. Restore's annual festival on the Elder Stubbs site in late August celebrating mental health and growing has become something of a local fixture.

The Elder Stubbs charity has another project with the local homelessness charity Steppin' Stones which includes an orchard as well as growing spaces.

Both charities use what they grow; to supply their kitchen in the case of Steppin' Stones, and their Cowley Road café and a local veg delivery service in the case of Restore. This tradition of growing at Restore can be traced back to the First World War when the land that is now Manzil Park and the adjoining health centre and housing estate were cultivated.

Growing in religious communities has a long and honourable tradition in east Oxford too, with the many orders that established themselves in the area from the 19th century, reframing and taking forward that tradition of sanctuary and hospitality into the present. The Society of All Saints Sisters of the Poor, based just off Cowley Road between Leopold Street and Magdalen Road are probably the best known contemporary example, with their pioneering Helen House, a hospice for children and a sanctuary for their parents and carers founded in 1982, followed more recently by Douglas House, a hospice for teenagers and young adults. As previously mentioned, the Cowley Fathers were great growers, ambitious too, with a large mulberry tree in the cloisters. One of their number, Fr Hollings, founded the Sisters of the Love of God Convent in 1911. Located on a five acre site

Horns of Plenty at the Elder Stubbs Festival.

running down to Meadow Lane behind Parker Street, the community of 26 nuns have an extensive kitchen garden, an orchard with over 80 trees, including apples, plums, cherries, pears and peaches and host two bee-keepers. The grounds are prolific and a large store for vegetables including squash, beetroot, and onions as well as for a huge variety of apples, ensure a practically year round supply of fresh produce for the community. Their honey, and juice from their apples is sold at the Farmers' Market by Tiddly-Pommes.

STILL A RADICAL ROAD

Cowley Road may have been gentrified in the past couple of decades and to many from other parts of the country might look relatively prosperous, but the area has had a history of poverty and exclusion right from that early leper colony at Bartlemas and the pilgrims and mendicants it attracted. As the suburb filled with college servants, artisans and labourers one observer in 1893 was still able to characterise some local residents as *'a residuum of the thriftless, careless, lazy ne'er-do-well sort whose nomadic instincts prevent them from settling to anything'.* In 1882 between 3–4,000 'tramps' were admitted to Cowley Road Workhouse and in 1908 an extraordinary 12,450 vagrants were reported to have stayed at least one night there.

Many of the memoirs and memories of Cowley Road from the turn of the 20th century are of struggling to get by, and there is no doubt that poverty is still pervasive, as the

Food Bank deliveries to refugee hostels and homelessness projects demonstrate. Soup kitchens (one in the old Workhouse chapel, now the Asian Cultural Centre), charities supplying free meals for homeless and vulnerable people and the high levels of take up of free school meals in some local schools are all testament to the fact that plenty of people in the Cowley Road area cannot afford to eat properly, ably documented in the recent report *'Feeding the Gaps'.* Hand-in-hand with poverty, though, have been defiance and resistance, from the bread riots of the 19th century and allotment rent strikes in the 20th century, to the more recent celebration and self-organisation of the Cowley Road Carnival.

SIGNPOSTS FOR THE FUTURE

Cowley Road is unique in many respects, but it is also a microcosm of wider society. A leader, a trailblazer in many ways, Cowley Road is also subject to the big shifts experienced in society as a whole. A proposed road scheme through east Oxford in the 1950s and 1960s engendered a blight on properties there (it came to nothing in the end) but that also provided opportunities for many, including immigrants to Britain who transformed the area into what it is today. The decline of the small neighbourhood shop in the face of supermarket competition has been a nationally-running theme which has in part been challenged in the Cowley Road area – hence its quirky uniqueness. But what next?

The years since the economic crash of 2008 in particular have seen shifts in society which have the potential to change Cowley Road and streets like it in unexpected, but often positive ways. One of the most striking themes to emerge from my interviews carried out in 2014 with shopkeepers and publicans, café and restaurant owners, local historians and commentators, has been a sense of a passing of an era: that the 'clone town' of high streets that look alike from Penzance to Inverness has, after years of valiant resistance, begun to arrive on Cowley Road too. There is some substance to this. Tesco has been joined by Morrisons and Sainsbury's, and chain takeaways and coffee shops although still a small minority, are now an established feature. Rising residential and commercial property prices are having an impact, as the London property boom ripples out to cities like Oxford. If houses in north Oxford can go for rents of £300,000 a year, the impact further down the chain is real, and independent businesses can get squeezed out by chains with deeper pockets.

SHIFTING SHOPPING HABITS

But the trends are by no means all one-way. One of the effects of the recession has been a change in the way people work. More work is part-time. There are many more self-employed people. (I am an example having been made redundant from public service in 2011.) They have less money to spend in shops but they are also under less pressure to cram a weekly food shop into a dash between work and the demands of the rest of life at an out-of-town superstore. Instead they can spend more time and think more about what they actually

Apples from Restore's orchard.

do need, rather than what they might need. This reversion to shopping lists, fewer impulse buys, more frequent local shopping trips and in some cases a focus on more locally produced food, is having an impact on shopping habits.

The impact on the supermarkets has been dramatic. Tesco have attempted to hide the vertiginous decline in profits from their shareholders by methods that are currently under investigation by the Serious Fraud Office. The £250m hole in their accounts revealed by a whistleblower in 2014 has led to a crisis of confidence in Britain's and Cowley Road's largest retailer that would have been unimaginable a year earlier. Fearsome price cutting has been one of the consequences – and corner cutting with it, as the horsemeat in beef burgers scandal in 2013 demonstrated.

The culture of shopping has shifted because frequent shopping trips with a shopping list means much less food is bought and wasted too. The Waste Resources Action Programme (WRAP) reports that domestic food waste has been cut by 21% in the past five years. That amounts to £13bn in lost revenue for grocery stores. No wonder their profits are looking sickly.

It has obvious financial benefits for households, but also environmental benefits and, of course, engenders a sense of social solidarity too. Who wants to be seen to be chucking out uneaten food when food banks are proliferating? One of the surprising things about all this is that it has been such a long time coming. 'Retail therapy' is a cliché but it refers to shopping as a leisure activity. Any retail mall sees shopping for clothes, shoes, home furnishings and the like as a trip out with friends and the opportunity for a social occasion, not shopping-as-chore. Yet until recently the supermarkets essentially sold food shopping in one of their big box stores as exactly that. Race round as fast as you can and spend as much as you can. And don't forget to fill up with petrol before you leave. Shame the petrol is so expensive these days and you need so much of it to get those 'value' items home.

Suddenly shopping in a range of local shops if only to supplement a range of online deliveries, seems far more attractive. No more congestion or fraught car journeys; instead keen prices, plenty of variety, the opportunity to catch up with your neighbours, meet a friend for a drink, walk the dog; the sociability of the market place, now that the office water cooler is perhaps not so readily available, connection with the shopkeepers and significant financial savings as the food bought actually gets eaten. What not to like? Not every town and city in England has the infrastructure to support this way of life. 'Clone town' developments and out-of-town superstores have certainly taken their toll in many, but for those which have successfully resisted those trends, the future looks brighter than it has for a while. I believe this to be the case for Cowley Road.

One other element in the food-as-leisure-activity trend is that of eating out. Recession changed shopping and eating habits, but the long-term trends towards eating out more and cooking at home less, haven't gone away. Nationally the construction of smaller houses with less space to eat in a kitchen and even in some cases insufficient space to store fresh produce, have helped drive this. Locally the rise in student numbers over the past decade or so has also accelerated this trend. If an area is attractive, and Cowley Road certainly is, going to the cinema, a live music event or some poetry in the upstairs room of a pub, can easily be combined with eating out. Cowley Road certainly offers variety and that variety has grown phenomenally in the last 20 years. The more variety, the more visitors. Suddenly eating out is the event in itself. This too reflects contradictory trends in society. Many are more careful about how they shop but eat out regularly as well; not in high-end restaurants but in the plethora of cheaper and take-away places.

ANYONE FOR CRICKETS?

So what will be new on the food scene on Cowley Road in the next few years? Food trends usually arrive slowly and take off suddenly. After all, Mrs Beeton knew about and used olive oil in the 1860s even if most people until the 1960s thought it was something you bought at the chemist to deal with ear wax. Now of course there is hardly a self-respecting household without a bottle in the kitchen. But global trends arrive and take root more quickly and in these days of increasing interest in the sustainability of food production my forecast of the

Street food in China, 2014.

next big thing is . . . insects. If Cowley Road's unique selling point is its cosmopolitan nature, with over 2 billion people world-wide eating insects (entomophagy) as part of their normal diet, it is only a matter of time before they arrive here. This came home to me on a month long solo trip to China in 2014 where crickets, grasshoppers, scorpions and many others are standard street food fare.

High protein, low carbon footprint and low production costs make them an attractive option, either salted and eaten as a snack with beer or as part of a more substantial meal – tempura grasshopper anybody? The recipes tend to have humorous names, Cricket McBuggetts, Chocolate chirp cookies. . . you get the picture.

If the Netherlands can embrace the consumption of insects, with Planet Organic now stocking them as the new 'superfood' and in 2015 with the Mexican street food chain Wahaca putting them on their menu for the first time in London, can Cowley Road be far behind?

CHAPTER FIVE

Contemporary Cowley recipes

The recipes that follow reflect the nature of Cowley Road and its history as well as my own cooking practice. They play to the Cowley Road area's strengths. In putting them together I have realised just how enjoyably mixed-up many of them are. Recipes with their origins in the Middle East, the Mediterranean, Southern and Eastern Europe, North Africa, the Caribbean, South Asia, North America and the Far East as well as those coming out of the whole food, and slow food (local, vegetarian and organic) movements are all represented. Some remain distinctly of those cultures but most have been adapted through being in Britain and specifically from being from Cowley Road, reflecting what I see as the 'terroir' of Cowley Road. Carmelina's account of her parents Joe and Anna Arucci's experience in making a success of La Capannina almost 50 years ago, in Chapter Three, is striking in this respect. The tradition of offering hospitality to the traveller, pilgrim, scholar or refugee, often unexpected or at short notice is something I try to reflect in this section.

COWLEY ROAD INSPIRED COOKING

The recipes are not gourmet and they are mostly pretty simple. Simple doesn't mean boring, but I do find some cookbooks and TV cooking shows irritatingly over-complicated or involving the use of extraordinarily expensive ingredients. And I have sought to evoke a particular place with my recipe selection, but inevitably it is a personal choice reflecting my own 'take' on the street and its character. The good news is it's possible to obtain all the items in the recipes locally, i.e. from Cowley Road and its environs, but some of them will be of poorer quality than can be obtained elsewhere (especially fish). However, trying to track some things down should be one of the joys of this book, exploring the deeper recesses of some of the shops that have perhaps just been names on the street up to now. There are many surprises to be had and many is the time I have come out of one food store

clutching something I barely knew existed, let alone had gone in with the intention of purchasing. My daughters survived my culinary explorations to tell the tale and still tease me about this.

ABOUT THE RECIPES

I have arranged the recipes by types of dishes, starting with *Soups, salads and snacks* (p68), *Breakfast and light meals* (p79), *Vegetarian main course* (p85), *Fish and meat main course* (p97), *Desserts* (p104) and finishing with *Preserves* (p112). In between you'll find something to whet your appetite from asparagus risotto to winter beetroot soup.

I hope you enjoy these flavours of my local street.

SOUPS, SALADS AND SNACKS

Soups can be made of just about anything (even mock turtles). The important point is to have good ingredients. Soups can be really chunky or pureed, in which case adding croutons or some cream is a good thing to do.

To my mind salads at their best are beautiful and useful at the same time. I have tried to suggest some different ways of 'doing' salad though the classics like tomato salad are still a favourite.

Snacks are great as something to take on a picnic or part of a packed lunch. They can even be expanded into a meal in themselves with some bread cheese, pickles or charcuterie.

SEE ALSO:

POTTAGE p11

MOCK TURTLE SOUP p19

WINTER BEETROOT SOUP

Serves 4

4 good-sized beetroot
3 carrots
2 sticks celery or a piece of celeriac
1 large onion
1 large potato
1 lemon
Small handful of parsley, chopped
Crème fraiche to taste

Wash all the vegetables. Boil the beetroot to soften the skin and then remove it, keeping the water for the soup base. Chop the onion finely and sauté in olive oil. Allow to lightly brown. Chop up the potato, carrot and other vegetable(s) and cook in the water, adding the onion. Grate or dice the beetroot (can be a messy job) and add to the other vegetables, topping up with water as required.

Simmer for 20–30 minutes. Add the juice of one lemon, remove from heat. Add 2 large spoonfuls of crème fraiche and the chopped parsley and serve with rye bread and pickles. (And vodka for authenticity.)

Beetroot is my favourite root vegetable. The farmers' market is good on different varieties. This works with any beetroot, but don't buy pink or golden varieties if you want a brilliant traditional red colour! My Polish friend Januz taught me this.

BEST FOR RUSSIAN AND
EASTERN EUROPEAN:
BALTIC FOODS
SOBIESKI MINI MARKET

BUTTERFLY SANCTUARY NETTLE SOUP

Serves 6

300 g nettle tips (first 6 leaves) – about a carrier bag full
1 large onion, chopped
1 large potato, cubed
2 cloves of garlic or
50 g wild garlic stems and leaves if you can find them
2 litres vegetable stock
75 g unsalted butter
1 sm bunch of chives for garnish
6 heaped tbsp crème fraiche
Salt and pepper

Place the potato, onion and garlic in a pan with the butter and sweat on a medium heat for 10 minutes, stirring. Add the vegetable stock and bring to the boil for 10 minutes. Using gloves, wash the nettles and discard the stalks. Add these and simmer for 5 minutesadding seasoning. Cool slightly and puree in batches. Return the soup to the pan and gently re heat. Ladle into bowls with a dollop of crème fraiche and a sprinkling of chives and further seasoning if desired. Horseradish sauce (see pxx) can be a substitute for crème fraiche. Serve with sourdough bread and salted goats butter.

This is a good spring foraging recipe. There are always nettles on allotment sites or paths and roadside verges – and a good thing too from the point of view of butterflies and other wildlife. I always enjoyed giving my daughters nettle soup when they were young. The frisson of eating something that stings. But it doesn't of course and it tastes lovely. The recipe can also use chickweed or fat hen as substitutes for nettle if you are into foraging.

BARTLEMAS ALLOTMENT SALAD

Serves 4+

Two handfuls each of oak leaf lettuce, little gem or cos lettuce, dandelion or Italian dandelion (for the lovely red ribbing) rocket, sorrel, young chard, spinach or beet leaves, lambs lettuce
One handful each of nasturtium leaves, basil, dill, parsley, chives and chicory
Plus tarragon, coriander or chervil, if you have them and 'poached egg plant' for foragers
2–3 spring onions thinly sliced
Flowers from courgettes, nasturtium and borage, plus petals from calendula (marigold) and blue geranium

Wash, dry and mix all these in a large salad bowl, keeping back some of the flowers to sprinkle on top. Visually they are a wonderfully appetising addition.

SALAD DRESSING
One tablespoon of balsamic or cider vinegar
4 tablespoons of olive oil
½ tsp of grain mustard
large pinch of salt, ground pepper.

Whisk together and add to salad. This goes very well with fresh bread, cheeses, hummus and olives.

My friend Eric who used to live on a boat on the canal with his family and has had an allotment forever, put this together and has a variation of it for nearly every month of the year. The point is to include whatever is available according to season. But this is typical.

Dressing is really important. The recipe below is a good basic, though some salads such as the potato one require a different approach. Olive oil is a staple and good quality does show through. I am particularly fond of the Palestinian Zaytoun (Fairtrade, organic).

WINTER KALE SALAD

Serves 4–6

Kale (as much or as little as you like)
Roughly grated Parmesan (use the carrot grater)
3 tsp minced shallots
4 tsp fresh lemon juice
1 tsp honey
1 tsp lemon zest
¾ tsp salt
¼ tsp ground black pepper
2 tbsp olive oil

Combine all the dressing ingredients and whisk robustly. Slice the kale very thinly and mingle in the dressing with your hands about 5 minutes before serving. As you serve, add a handful of Parmesan and toss gently.

This is a really interesting salad to have in winter when traditional salad ingredients are harder to find (or less appetising). Most people assume kale has to be cooked. It doesn't. Providing it is young and fresh, kale is lovely raw when chopped finely. It is of course the modern British cuisine 'superfood' of choice these days.

BEST FOR KALE AND SIMILAR:
CULTIVATE VEG VAN

BROAD BEAN AND MUSHROOM SALAD

Serves 4

250 g shelled fresh broad beans
200 g chestnut mushrooms
150 g chanterelle mushrooms
75 g walnuts broken or roughly chopped
Juice of one lemon
75 ml olive oil
1 tbsp white wine or cider vinegar
½ tsp ground cumin
1 tsp chopped marjoram

The mushrooms are marinaded in this recipe, not cooked. Chop or slice the mushrooms into pieces that 'go' with the broad beans, so perhaps halve the chestnut mushrooms, or slice if large. Whisk up the marinade with the olive oil, vinegar and lemon juice plus a little salt. Pour over the mushrooms in a good-sized bowl, mixing the mushrooms well, and leave for 1 hour. Having podded the broad beans (actually very small ones can be eaten pod and all) cook them in boiling water for about 2–3 minutes. Drain and allow to cool. Add the broad beans, walnuts and cumin to the mushrooms, sprinkle with the marjoram and some pepper and serve perhaps with a dollop of Greek yoghurt per serving.

I often get asked what my favourite vegetable is. Asparagus comes to mind, but it has such a short season and Oxford's clay soil doesn't make it the easiest thing to grow. So I usually say beetroot or broad beans. I'm also something of a mushroom fan, though I've only grown them at home a couple of times. There are plenty in the wild (if you know what you are picking!) and in the shops.

FRESH-FROM-THE-TREE FIG SALAD

Serves 6

12 fresh ripe figs
1 bunch fresh green basil
1 bunch fresh purple basil
6 balls of mozzarella
Juice of 2 lemons
Olive oil
Salt and pepper

Wash the figs if you have bought them. Then cut off the stems and then quarter the figs. Separate the basil leaves from stalks and flower heads. Wash and shake dry. Take the mozzarella out of any liquid and dry with kitchen towel. Tear up each ball into 4–5 pieces. Place the figs and mozzarella pieces onto a large serving plate so that they look pretty. Scatter the 2 sorts of basil leaves over them (if you only have green that is fine). Mix the lemon juice with 3 times its volume in olive oil. Add the salt and pepper. Pour over the plate and serve immediately, outside with some chilled white wine.

I had a lot of fun with this recipe when I first made it in 2013. In fact I blogged about it. It is adapted from Rose Gray and Ruth Rodgers *River Café Green* and it is one of those recipes I never imagined I'd be able to do in England. That summer was a particularly fruitful one and figs were no exception. I got over 170 off my fig tree in the garden. The basil was equally luxuriant, so this recipe was crying out to be made. A wonderful whiff of the Mediterranean.

BEST FOR CHEESE:
FARMERS' MARKET
IL PRINCIPE

POTATO SALAD

Serves 6

800 g new or salad potatoes
A dozen quails' eggs (You can of course use fresh hens' eggs
instead, say 3–4; slice or quarter them after peeling)
150 g peas (smallish), fresh or frozen
½ jar pesto, home-made (recipe p113) or shop bought
½ tsp white wine vinegar
Bunch of mint finely shredded
A little parsley, chopped or capers

Wash the potatoes. Leave the skins on. Boil for 5–7 minutes or so
– depending on size, until cooked. Boil the quails' eggs. They take
one minute for soft and 2 minutes for hard boiled. Hard boiled are
definitely easier to peel. Run in cold water and peel. Boil the peas for
one minute. Drain, allow to cool. Once the potatoes are cooked, drain
them, run some cold water over them and cut them in 2, or smaller
pieces if strange shapes like pink fir apple. Put in a large bowl and
toss with the pesto, mint, peas and vinegar, mixing well so that the still
warm potatoes absorb the flavours. Cut the eggs in half and mix them
in too. Garnish with the parsley or capers if you like them and plenty
of pepper.

This is a salad to celebrate salad potatoes. Strangely, professional cookery writers in the main don't seem to know very much about potato varieties, going into loving detail on different kinds of cheese or pasta variety but just referring to potatoes as 'floury' or 'new'. Charlotte, Ratte or Pink Fir Apple are the best for this. These make a great summer salad – very portable on a picnic and the eggs add a bit of class.

BEST FOR POTATO VARIETIES:
CULTIVATE VEG VAN

GREEK SALAD

Serves 4

10 small sweet tomatoes
1 chilled cucumber
25 kalamata olives (best with stone in)
½ a red onion
150 g feta cheese – making sure it's reasonably dry and crumbly
1 tbsp capers
3 sprigs fresh oregano roughly chopped (dried is okay)
6 tbsp olive oil
2 tbsp red wine vinegar
salt and grain mustard for the dressing of your choice.

Optional: 1 sm cos lettuce Some fresh fennel Some green olives to add to the black ones Whole small radishes

Wrap feta in kitchen towel to remove moisture if necessary. Slice the onion really thinly in the salad bowl. Chop the cucumber and tomatoes into chunks and add. Then add the olives, capers, oregano and if you are including them, the Cos lettuce leaves torn, radishes and fennel, finely sliced. Finally add the feta cheese broken into chunks or crumbled. Mix in with the salad dressing and serve with crispy bread, cheese or whatever else you are eating, sardines for example.

This is a classic that can't be ignored, even if one well known TV chef has described it as 'an abominable fixture in the culinary canon'. Yes it is simple and like all simple recipes it is endlessly versatile, but of course mucking about with the basic principles – 'cold and salty' – ruins it. This is the basic recipe made in our household hundreds of times, to which a few things can be added according to taste and availability.

BEST FOR OLIVES:
IL PRINCIPE

COWLEY ROAD-STYLE MEZE

There is absolutely no reason why you should stick to Mediterranean or Middle Eastern ingredients. Mix up the tradition with onion bhaji, samosas, or for a touch of the eastern European, throw in some sliced hard boiled eggs, pickled gherkins, saukraut, mushrooms or leftover potato salad. Here is a suggestion for a fairly traditional meze; all ingredients readily found on Cowley Road. The world on a plate.

Hummus, chickpeas and tahini dip (recipe given below)
Babaganoush, garlicky lemony aubergine dip
Ttzatsiki, cucumber and yoghurt dip
Gigantes, extra large butter beans in a tomato sauce
Makdous, whole small aubergines stuffed with walnuts and chilli
Za'atar, dried mixture of crushed fragrant herbs such as thyme, mixed with sumac, roasted sesame seeds and salt (best eaten with bread dipped in olive oil)
Black and green olives, perhaps mixed with feta cubes

Serve these with warmed pitta bread, crusty brown bread and a small dish of that Palestinian olive oil for dipping the breads into.

Meze is a very common dish for sharing throughout the Mediterranean and Middle East. There are almost endless permutations and Cowley Road can provide all the ingredients for something really special. Because of this I'm going to cheat a bit and suggest that the whole of this dish can be bought from shops and assembled at home, rather than you trying to make it yourself. They can almost certainly make most of it better than you can and it is much quicker.

BEST FOR MEZE
INGREDIENTS:
MELI
MAROC DELI
EASTERN AND
CONTINENTAL STORES

HUMMUS

This is such an easy thing to make and can be used in picnics, packed lunches or as part of a meze above.

2 tins of chickpeas drained and rinsed (approx 480 g)
½ a jar of tahini (approx 4 tbsp)
3 tbsp olive oil
3–4 cloves garlic
Juice of one lemon
1 tsp salt

Whizz up the chickpeas, lemon, garlic and a little water in a food mixer until they make a fairly smooth paste. Tip into a bowl and add the tahini, olive oil and salt. Stir together. If it is a bit too stiff add a little more water, lemon juice or olive oil to taste. Put in serving bowl and put in the fridge for 15 minutes. Before serving, garnish with a sprinkling of paprika, pine nuts and a little olive oil on the surface, or a few cooked chickpeas (optional).

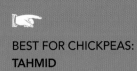

BEST FOR CHICKPEAS:
TAHMID

BREAKFASTS AND LIGHT MEALS

'All day breakfast' is one of the signs that cafés put out as a sure fire winner and Cowley Road is no exception. The British do love their breakfast – whatever time of the day it is. Traditionally it is safe and predictable.

The 'full English' is the stuff of legends. Some of my Airbnb guests arrive with only three or four phrases in English. 'Full English' is always one of them. None of these would be what they have in mind, but to be fair they do enjoy the experiments I have tried on them too. Such charming English eccentricity. Well worth a photo to send home.

SEE ALSO:

OXFORD SAUSAGE p25

COTSWOLD CRUNCH p31

ORIGINAL UHURU MUESLI p57

KEDGEREE

Serves 4

500 g sustainable smoked haddock
2–3 fresh free range eggs, hard boiled, peeled and quartered
450 g brown rice (or basmati rice)
1 large onion 1 green chilli, de-seeded and chopped
1 tsp curry powder
150 g butter
Handful of chives, chopped
Small bunch of coriander of flat leaf parsley, chopped
½ lemon, cut into four wedges

Wash the rice and place in a large pan with 600 ml boiling water. Brown rice takes longer to cook than basmati and may need topping up with water. Cover and cook for 35 minutes. Place the fish skin-side-up in a shallow pan over a low heat and cover in a 50/50 mix of water and milk. Bring to the boil and cook for 5 minutes. Allow to sit and cool and them remove the skin and break the flesh into large flakes. Melt the butter in a frying pan, add the onion, fry until softened and stir in the chilli and curry powder. Cook for a couple of minutes. Then add the fish stock and stir in the rice – having fluffed it up first and allow the mixture to coat and meld together. Then add the fish flakes and chopped eggs and stir gently. Scatter the chives and coriander on top and serve with the lemon wedges.
I suggest serving with Assam tea.

Kedgeree is the kind of breakfast made when honoured guests from the other side of the country are visiting. For me it also brings back memories of holidays on the Norfolk coast or the Isle of Wight with my grandparents, in rather formal but slightly down-at-heel hotels where it was a bit exotic and also generally rather too dry.

CHANNA DHAL AND PANEER

Serves 4

225 g channa dal or yellow split peas
225 g tomatoes chopped
1 small onion, chopped
2 small green chillis, de-seeded and finely chopped
30 g fresh root ginger, peeled and finely chopped
2 tsp cumin seeds
1 tsp garam masala
1 tsp ground turmeric
2 tsp brown sugar
2 tbsp raisins soaked in water for ½ hour and drained
30 gms dried or fresh coconut
60 g butter
Salt to taste

Optional:
150 g yoghurt
200 g paneer, chopped into cubes
A little fresh coriander, chopped

Add the channa dal to a small pan of boiling water. Cook for 30 minutes. Drain and run cold water over it. Mash it. Heat half the butter on a medium heat in a large pan. Add the onion and cumin and cook for 3–4 minutes. Add the ginger, chilli, garam masala, turmeric seeds and sugar and cook for a couple more minutes, stirring. Add the dhal, chopped tomatoes and salt to taste, stirring it all together and allow to cook until tender. Heat the remaining butter in a small frying pan, add the coconut and raisins and fry until golden. Pour onto the dhal. Serve with paneer cubes garnished with chopped coriander, or a spoonful of yoghurt per helping.

I was working in Bhopal, India in the mid 1980s with the trade unions and civic groups campaigning to get justice for those affected by the world's worst industrial accident, from Union Carbide (they are still waiting 30 years later) and was fed this regularly. I was living with local families so I never had to cook this in India. It takes time to cook so don't think of this as a quick breakfast. This is a slightly anglicised version. I used to eat it with paneer, which is a kind of Indian halloumi cheese which comes in cubes. Best go out and buy them.

BEST FOR SOUTH ASIAN:
TAHMID STORES
EASTERN AND
CONTINENTAL STORES
NOOR

SCRAMBLED EGGS AND MUSHROOMS

Serves 4

8 large fresh free-range eggs
100–150 g of your favourite mushrooms – chanterelle,
ceps or chestnut
80 g butter
4 slices of bread, toasted and buttered
A good splash of milk

Break the eggs into a dish and beat thoroughly. Take the mushrooms, slice fairly finely and put in a frying pan with half the butter. Cook slowly. Heat the other half the butter gently in a good-sized pan. Pour in the egg mixture and the milk. Turn up the heat a little and stir briskly with a wooden spoon making sure the egg doesn't stick to the bottom of the pan. Put the scrambled eggs on the toast and put the mushrooms on the scrambled egg. Garnish with a little bit of chopped flat leaf parsley. If you want to add something more substantial to the dish add a couple of Oxford sausages per serving.

Scrambled eggs are my favourite way of eating eggs for breakfast. In the 1980s I was active as an adult leader in Woodcraft Folk and on one occasion as KP (in charge of the kitchens) I decided to cook it for breakfast – for 88 people. Fortunately not camping, but in an outdoor pursuits centre with appropriately sized pans. It was a triumph and I never looked back. As a hen keeper for the past 15 years I have had plenty of opportunity to turn freshly laid eggs into scrambled egg. Popular with my Airbnb guests too.

BEST FOR DRIED
MUSHROOMS:
IL PRINCIPE

BEST FOR BOTTLED
MUSHROOMS:
BALTIC FOODS

ELDERFLOWER FRITTATA

Serves 4

8 fresh free-range eggs
1 cup of elderflowers, freshly picked
The finely grated zest of one lemon
2 tbsp of plain flour
2 tbsp olive oil
50 g caster sugar (optional)
Pinch of salt
1 lemon, quartered

Remove all the stems from the flowers, a bit of a fiddly business. Beat the eggs well. Add the olive oil to a large frying pan and then add the elderflowers and heat gently. Pour in the eggs, flour, lemon zest and half the sugar and fry until the underside forms a crust and the top is nearly solid.

Serve cut into slices with the lemon quarters and the rest of the sugar sprinkled on top. The sugar goes well with elderflowers and lemon but it is optional.

I have several elder trees on the back of my allotment. Elderflowers really are one of the gifts of nature, with a glorious smell that can be captured in elderflower cordial or champagne and released in winter. I like this recipe because the eggs are fresh from my hens and elderflowers can be picked in 5 minutes. It makes a lovely early summer breakfast. If you want to try this in Spring you can substitute apple blossom for elderflowers.

BEST FOR EGGS:
**ALDERS
FARMERS' MARKET**

STOTTIE CAKE

I couldn't resist including this eponymous recipe. Serves 2

550 g strong white flour
1½ teaspoons salt
15 g caster sugar
1 sachet dried yeast
30 g lard
350 ml warm water

Mix the flour, salt, sugar and yeast together in a bowl. Rub in the fat and then make into a stiff dough with the warm water. Turn it out onto a floured board and knead until smooth, about ten minutes. Place in an oiled bowl, cover with a dishcloth, and leave to rise in a warm place for about an hour, until well risen.

Divide into 2 (stottie cakes are supposed to be large, like focaccia, not like baps) and make each piece into a flat disc about 20 cm in diameter using a rolling pin. Place on an oiled baking sheet and allow to rise for about 15 minutes. Create a series of dimples on the top with your fingers. Then place in a pre-heated oven at 200°c/gas mark 6 for 12–15 minutes.

Cool on a wire rack, cut in half to make 2 disc shaped halves, and fill with your favourite sandwich fillings.

'Stotting' is a Geordie term for bouncing as in 'It's raining cats and dogs; it's stotting off the pavement.' Stottie cake is a white bread baked on the bottom of a coal fired oven and is confined to the north east of England. It is essentially an English focaccia bread (both are styled 'hearth breads') and it is strange that it hasn't become more popular. As with focaccia, it is ideal to fill with all kinds of interesting ingredients, traditionally bacon and pease pudding, but cream cheese, anchovies and salad leaves are good, and so is mozzarella, pesto and sundried tomatoes.

BEST FOR BREAD AND FLOWERS:
GIBBONS BAKERY
GERMAN BAKERY VAN
FARMERS' MARKET

VEGETARIAN MAIN COURSE

Good cooking is about fresh local seasonal ingredients, organic whenever possible, used thoughtfully. This is hardly an original insight of mine – indeed Rose Gray and Ruth Rodgers say something very like it in the introduction to their book *River Café Cook Book Green* and it is the principle the Slow Food Movement is based upon. That is why I have concentrated on fresh vegetables as a focus running through these recipes, especially as there are so many good sources in greengrocers up and down Cowley Road, the farmers' market, the Cultivate 'veg van' on-line ordering service and of course allotments and gardens for those who have access to them. Some of these recipes use fruit and vegetables which stray a little beyond the standard range, but they don't go for the really exotic. All of these are ones I have enjoyed over the years from east Oxford sources.

SEE ALSO:

END OF THE WORLD STEW p56

ASPARAGUS RISOTTO

Serves 4

600 g fresh asparagus chopped into bite-sized pieces
250 g Carnaroli risotto rice (Arborio is fine, but it has a tendency
to break up in cooking)
1 tbsp parsley leaves, chopped
1 onion, chopped
80 g parmesan cheese
2 vegetable stock cubes
100 g butter
3 tbsp olive oil
1.3 litres water

One of the really great things about risotto is that there are so many possible variations. My daughter became something of a risotto queen and the versions produced never disappointed. This asparagus one can be adapted for use with beans, tomatoes, mushrooms or just plain with fresh herbs and some lemon. Adding a little wine is a good idea, white in this case, but red for mushrooms or if you have it to hand or just prefer it. Asparagus is easy to get hold of in season (though I really do not recommend buying it if it has been imported from distant lands) and this was an enjoyable father/daughter joint project as I could contribute super-fresh allotment asparagus.

Gently soften the onion in a large pan with the oil and half the butter. Add the stock to the water in a separate pan and bring to a simmer. Grate the parmesan. Add the rice and half of the parsley to the onions and stir to coat the grains. Add the stock to the rice a ladleful at a time and allow it to be more or less absorbed before adding the next. Add the chopped asparagus late in the process – about 5 minutes or so from the end. Add the wine too. After about 20 minutes take it off the heat, add the remaining butter, parsley and parmesan cheese (reserving a little for sprinkling on top) and stir vigorously. Add salt and pepper to taste and serve.

MEJADARRA

Serves 4–5

250 g puy lentils
250 g brown rice
4 medium onions, cut finely
6 cloves garlic
250 ml olive oil
1 tsp coriander seeds
1 tsp cumin seeds
1 tsp turmeric
3–4 cardamom seeds
3–4 fenugreek seeds
3 cloves
2 bay leaves
1 star anise
½ cinnamon stick
½ a glass of sherry
250 ml yoghurt
750 ml water

Wash and then soak the lentils for 3 hours. Soak the rice for 30 minutes and then wash. Roast the coriander and cumin seeds and crush. Put the lentils in a large pan and stir fry with half the oil for 2–3 minutes. Add most of the water, bring to the boil, reduce and simmer for 15 minutes. Fry the onions in the remaining oil. Add the spices and the rice to the lentils with the rest of the water and simmer until the lentils and the rice are tender and all the water is absorbed; about 20 minutes. Add the sherry. Tip the lentils and rice into a serving bowl, mix in ¾ of the onions, pour the yoghurt over it and garnish with the remaining onions.

Serve with salad and olives.

This is a dish that has its origins in the Middle East. My friend Samia from Palestine introduced it to me and she has added some items that wouldn't be found in the traditional version. In Palestine it was traditionally made in November around the time of the olive harvest, because it uses a lot of olive oil.

BEST FOR MIDDLE EASTERN:
MAROC DELI
EASTERN AND
CONTINENTAL STORES
GREEN VILLAGE

This is simple yet incredibly tasty. It is a reliable vegetarian 'treat meal' too.

BEST FOR VEGETABLES:
SIMPLI FRESH
CULTIVATE VEG VAN
MAROC DELI

STUFFED PEPPERS

Serves 4

4 red peppers
4 green peppers
4 yellow peppers
3 potatoes, thinly sliced
1 kg tomatoes
400 g white rice
Small bunch spring onions, chopped
Bunch flat-leaf parsley, chopped
3 tbsp sumac
1 tsp cinnamon
1 tsp allspice
400 ml olive oil
1 litre water
2 lemons, juiced

Use a large baking dish or 2 smaller ones. Pre heat the oven to 200°c/gas mark 6. Make sure the peppers are of even size and have flat enough bases that they can stand up. Cut the tops off the peppers and remove the core carefully including the seeds. Pour some of the olive oil into the dish and line it with the 3 thinly sliced tomatoes. Then add the potatoes.

For the stuffing, rinse the rice, drain and put in a bowl. Dice the rest of the tomatoes and add along with the spring onions and parsley. Season with the sumac, cinnamon and allspice, mix in with the lemon juice and the rest of the olive oil. Mix well. Taste and add seasoning if necessary. Fill each pepper about ¾ full. Then add some water to each, about 50 ml. Put their tops on and pour the rest of the water over the potatoes and tomatoes. Bake for 1½ hours. Check after 1 hour. If it looks as if it is drying out add some more water and/or cover with aluminium foil.

PASTA WITH BROAD BEANS

Serves 4

300 g pasta shapes (penne, fusilli)
1 small onion, finely chopped
600 g broad beans, podded or equivalent in other veg
e.g. a whole head of broccoli or a whole medium cabbage
(savoy is great because it is crinkly)
2–3 garlic cloves, sliced
6 tbsp olive oil
Large pinch chilli flakes
Parmesan cheese, grated

Pod the beans, or prepare the greens by removing thick stalks and shredding the leaves or cut the broccoli into small florets. Heat the olive oil over a low heat and cook the onion and garlic for 10 minutes. Add the chill a couple of minutes before the end.

Boil water for the pasta and get it going in a large pan. About 3 minutes before it is cooked add the greens. Drain the pasta and greens thoroughly and add to the onion mixture in the pan. If you want to bulk up the meal add a tin of drained chickpeas at this point. Toss the mixture together in the frying pan.

Serve with plenty of grated parmesan and a little extra olive oil.

The thing I like about this recipe is that it is both Italian and British. Traditionally everyone, including me, cooks pasta with Mediterranean-type vegetables. But you don't have to and pasta goes very well with other fresh veg like cabbage, kale, broccoli or my favourite, broad beans depending on the season. It is adapted from a recipe by Hugh Fearnley-Whittingstall. Traditionally pasta recipes have lots of pasta with veg on top or mixed in. This reverses the proportions.

--

BEST FOR PASTA:
IL PRINCIPE

VEGETARIAN TAGINE AND COUSCOUS

Serves 4

1 large butternut squash (about 1 kg) peeled, seeds scooped out
and cut into bite sized chunks
400 g shallots, peeled and halved or 1 large onion, chopped
2 red peppers, de-seeded and cut into chunks
2 small/ medium potatoes, quartered or 2 large carrots, chopped
10–12 pitted prunes • 450 ml vegetable stock
1 tsp turmeric • 1 tsp ground cumin • 1 tsp cinnamon
2 tbsp olive oil • 1 tbsp clear honey
Handful fresh coriander (or parsley), chopped
Handful fresh mint, chopped • Juice of one lemon

For couscous:
250 g couscous
1 400 g tin chickpeas, drained and rinsed
1 tbsp harissa • Handful toasted flaked almonds, or pine nuts

Fry the shallots in the oil in a large pan for 5 minutes until softened
and browned. Add the squash and potato and the spices and stir
for one minute. Pour in the stock, season well and add the prunes,
lemon juice and honey. Cover and simmer for 8–10 minutes. Add the
peppers and cook for a further 8– 10 minutes until tender. Stir in the
coriander and most of the mint.

For the couscous. Pour 400 ml of boiling water over the couscous in a
bowl and stir in the harissa. Tip in the chickpeas and cover and leave
for 5 minutes. Fluff up with a fork and serve with the tagine, flaked
almonds and the remaining mint. If the troops are hungry, add a plate
of warmed pitta bread.

Tagines are fun because they are one of those dishes that is so versatile. This is the vegetarian version, but there are of course meat-ball, chicken or lamb varieties. They are something you can cook when you don't really feel like cooking and teenagers will fall on it and be complimentary when they have demolished the lot. This is a classic recipe where it is 'the point of departure' rather than a closely worked out plan. Vegetables and spices can be substituted pretty freely. If you have an ingredient use it, if you don't, don't worry nobody will complain.

BEST FOR FRESH HERBS:
EASTERN AND
CONTINENTAL
SIMPLI FRESH

ROASTED SQUASH

Serves 6

1 large (1 kg) butternut squash, pumpkin or similar
8 garlic cloves (skin on)
5 tbsp olive oil
2–3 sprigs rosemary
Pinch chilli flakes
Salt

Heat the oven to 200°c/ gas mark 6. Slice the squash into quarters and scoop out the seeds. Keep the skin on. Chop the squash into wedges and place in a roasting tie adding the garlic, cloves, rosemary and chilli flakes. Pour the olive oil over it all, toss it and roast for 45 minutes turning over the squash a couple of times to make sure it is all cooked, soft and slightly caramelised on the edges.

This is ready to eat on its own, or with couscous, risotto or something nutty like walnuts or pine nuts mixed in at the end.

I love this recipe because squash and pumpkins never come in small quantities. Either the ones you get in shop are large or if you grow your own a lot seem to come at once and while they store well enough they always feel like you should make a big deal of them. They aren't a side dish – although they do go well with other things as well as on their own.

This is a classic Greek dish. But I associate it with a certain American style of cooking exemplified in Mollie Katzen's *The Enchanted Broccoli Forest*, a bible for the hippie aspirant gourmet (if that isn't a contradiction in terms). Anyway it has been a family staple for years. The fact that it uses a lot of spinach is a real plus. It is possible to make your own filo pastry but it is just as good to buy it. Meli sell a good version of spanakopita if you don't want to cook it yourself.

SPANAKOPITA

Serves 4–5

1 kg Spinach rinsed and chopped • 1 large onion, chopped
2 cloves garlic crushed • 30 g parsley chopped
2 free-range eggs • 250 g feta cheese • 125 g ricotta cheese
3 tbsp olive oil • 8–10 sheets filo pastry
1 tbsp sesame seeds
Nutmeg, preferably freshly grated, to taste
100 g butter, melted • 3 tbsp olive oil
Salt and pepper

Pre-heat the oven to 180°c/gas mark 4. Make sure the filo pastry is not frozen. Lightly oil a large baking tin. Heat the olive oil in a large frying pan, to a medium heat and sauté the onions and garlic. Cook the spinach and parsley in a pan until the spinach is limp; 3–5 minutes. Drain into a colander and press down with a wooden spoon to get rid of excess liquid. Add to the onion and garlic and mix in the nutmeg. Set aside to cool. In a medium sized bowl, beat the eggs and add the ricotta and feta, crumbling as you go along. Stir it into the spinach mixture once it has drained and cooled a little.

Lay a sheet of filo pastry in the prepared baking dish and brush lightly with butter. Repeat with three or four more sheets. The sheets will overhang the dish. Spread the spinach and cheese mixture into the tin and fold over any overhanging filo. Then lay the remaining four or 5sheets to the top one at a time, brushing each one with butter as you proceed. Tuck any overhanging filo into the tin to seal the filling. Add a final brush of butter on top and scatter sesame seeds and some sea salt, and bake for 35–40 minutes until golden brown.

CELARIAC AND POTATO MASH (AND OXFORD SAUSAGES)

Serves 6

2 kg Wilja potatoes or similar mashers, peeled and cut into chunks
1 kg celeriac, peeled and cubed
3 garlic cloves, crushed
2 sprigs flat leaf parsley, finely chopped
1 litre whole milk
100 g butter Salt and pepper to tast

Cook the potatoes in a large pan of water for about 15 minutes until soft enough to mash. Drain and leave in a colander. Bring the milk to the boil in a pan add the celeriac and simmer until soft, about 15 minutes. Puree the celeriac in a food processor with the butter and about 300 ml of the hot milk. Add the parsley and put in a warmed large bowl. Add most of the remaining milk to the potatoes and mash purposively until smooth. Add the celeriac and beat in until well combined, adding a little more butter or milk as you go along until you get the consistency you like.

Season and serve with a couple of Oxford sausages per person.

In some ways this is the most surprising recipe in the book, because the ingredients look so ordinary sitting on the kitchen table, but the result is divine! You need good mashing potatoes like Wilja. As far as I am concerned this is about as close as you will get to an Oxford 'signature dish', as you can add Oxford sausages to your mash and even substitute horseradish sauce to the mashed potato, instead of, or even as well as, the celeriac and add a marmalade glaze to the sausages.

ALLOTMENT COURGETTE AND TOMATO TIAN

Serves 6+

1 kg courgettes (not too big)
1 kg ripe tomatoes
2 medium onions sliced
2 peppers de seeded and sliced
4–5 cloves garlic, roughly chopped, or whole if small
2 sprigs thyme
100 ml olive oil (may need more if you like it)
50 ml tomato puree
A dash of red wine

Pre-heat the oven to 200°c/gas mark 6. Slice up the onions and peppers. Heat up some olive oil in a large frying pan, add the peppers and onions and cook until they are softened and beginning to colour. Then add the garlic, mix together and spread the mixture over the base of the dish.

Thinly slice the tomatoes, top and tail the courgettes and cut into thin diagonal slices. Lay them in alternate rows on the base. Mix the wine, olive oil and tomato puree and add to this tian with the thyme. Put in the oven and cook for 30–40 minutes, by which time it should have darkened at the edges. Remove and allow to cool slightly while you barbeque your fish or meat. Alternatively eat with some fresh bread, ideal for soaking up the juices. Finish the wine you started for the tian.

I find that courgettes and tomatoes seem to come in abundance on the allotment in the late summer. They cry out to be eaten in quantity fresh from the plot. Cook in a large dish so it can be easily served outside on a summer evening. If you have some kind of barbeque, this goes well with some pieces of fish or chicken cooked on it.

SZECHWAN TOFU AND AUBERGINE

Serves 4

1 large aubergine, cut into thin strips lengthwise and quartered
1 medium onion
8 spring onions, green ends separated, white ends chopped
1 bunch fresh coriander, roughly chopped
350 g tofu (drained weight), cut into strips. Tempeh cut into thin strips is a very good substitute
2 tbsp peanut oil
4 cloves garlic, crushed
1 tbsp grated fresh ginger
1 tsp cayenne pepper
75 ml dry sherry or Chinese rice wine
50 ml soy sauce
1 tbsp cider vinegar
3 tbsp cornflour

Combine the soy sauce, sherry, and vinegar with water to make 250 ml liquid. Mix in the cornflour and dissolve. Heat a large wok over a high flame. Add the oil and onion and stir fry for one minute. Add the aubergine pieces and stir fry for 8–10 minutes until soft. Add the garlic, ginger, cayenne pepper and salt and pepper to taste and cook for a couple more minutes. Add the tofu and chopped spring onions. Turn down the heat slightly, whisk up the liquid and add while stirring, cooking for a further few minutes until the liquid is reduced to a thick sauce.

Serve with rice or noodles topped with the coriander and chopped spring onion greens.

Apart from muesli, tofu is probably the most readily parodied of all the foods taken up by the wholefood movement. But of course it has a long an honourable tradition in Chinese cooking and is readily available in Chinese and East Asian shops.

BEST FOR TOFU:
JING JING
UHURU

The thing about a vegetable tart is that you can make it at any time of the year with the vegetables available and it will always taste good. The exact mix of veg therefore doesn't really matter. Include what you like eating. This is a Mediterranean veg version, but leek and potato is also very good.

ROAST VEGETABLE TART

Serves 4

1 small courgette, diced
1 red pepper and one green pepper de-seeded and sliced into strips • 1 medium aubergine, diced• 2 medium onions, thinly sliced • 8 cherry tomatoes, halved• 300g short crust pastry 100 ml olive oil • 100 g goats cheese • 100 g ricotta 3–4 sprigs of thyme • 2 medium free range eggs 200 ml double cream

Pre-heat the oven to 230°c/gas mark 8. Roast the peppers by putting them in an oven-proof dish at the top of the oven for 10 minutes with some olive oil. Add the courgette and aubergine, stirring to make sure they are covered in olive oil. Return to the oven for another 10 minutes.

Meantime sauté the onions for 15 minutes while they turn soft and brown. Remove the veg from the oven, turn it down to 160°c/gas mark 3. Lightly grease a large (22 inch approx) loose-bottomed tart tin. Roll out the pastry into a circle roughly 3 cm thick and carefully place it in the tin (no holes in the pastry) and line the pastry case with a large sheet of baking paper. Put baking beans (I use dried chickpeas) in and blind-bake for 30 minutes. Remove the paper with the beans and bake for about another 10 minutes. Remove and allow to cool. Scatter the base of the tart with the onions and cover with the roasted vegetables. Scatter half the thyme over it, add the cheese in pieces and the cherry tomatoes cut side up.

Whisk the eggs and cream in a small bowl, add salt and pepper and carefully pour the mix into the tart, making sure the vegetables and cheese are still visible. Scatter the remaining thyme and cook for 30 minutes. When it looks a golden colour remove and allow to rest for 10 minutes before taking out of the tin and serving with baked potatoes and a green salad.

FISH AND MEAT MAIN COURSE

Fresh fish is in short supply in east Oxford. It is a long way from the sea, but just as important I suspect is that fish is seen as 'difficult' to cook. Hopefully these recipes will dispel that idea. The best supplier of fresh fish in Oxford is Hayman's in the Covered Market who also do a fish cash and carry on Osney Mead in west Oxford with a huge range of fresh and sustainable fish – by far the best source of fish in Oxfordshire. There is a good fish stall at the farmers' market which sells local trout but no other species and Tesco do sell some pre-packaged fish. Otherwise fish on Cowley Road is frozen or dried, though the range in Asian supermarkets is surprisingly wide.

SEE ALSO:

POACHED RIVER FISH p15

FRIED HADDOCK AND CHIPS p37

MACH BAJA BANGLADESHI FISH p51

I have selected a number of game dishes because as a non-meat eater it seems to me to be a much less intensive way of eating meat. Game is also quite readily available and a little goes a long way. Alder's has by far the best range. John Maynard Keynes is said to have fed a Bloomsbury Group dinner party 3 grouse between 11 guests, an act of stinginess that delighted Vanessa Bell, her eyes gleaming 'as the bones went round'. Perhaps he wasn't very good at estimating quantities, but these recipes will help if you are unfamiliar with game.

SEE ALSO:

ROAST GOOSE p16

OXFORD SAUSAGE p25

HAND OF PORK p35

OSSOBUCO MILANESE p39

MOUSSAKA p41

PERM PELMENI p47

MERGUEZ PAELLA p49

GRIDDLED MACKEREL

Serves 4

2 large or 4 small mackerel, filleted
4 large desiree potatoes (or other good baking varieties)
3–4 tbsp rapeseed oil
1 lemon, cut into wedges
Butter

Bake the potatoes in the oven whole or cut in half. Depending on size and whether you pre-cook them in a microwave first, they are likely to take 35–40 minutes. If you want to try this on the beach pierce the potatoes, wrap them in tinfoil and place them in the embers of your campfire. Allow 10 minutes longer if cooking in foil. When my daughters were little they referred to these jacket potatoes as 'baked potatoes in their coats'.

Heat a griddle pan with the oil till it is hot and just smoking. Take the fish and rub a small amount of butter over the flesh. Griddle them skin side down for 3 minutes. They should sizzle immediately. Reduce the heat a little. Turn them over and do the flesh side for a further 2–3 minutes.

Serve with lemon wedges, and the baked potatoes with butter and a green salad.

Ever since I was a child catching them off the side of a boat or the jetty on holiday, I've loved mackerel. So beautiful. Cooking over a fire on the beach is a treasured holiday memory. Just as well that they are still considered sustainable (Icelandic and Faeroese apart) and so good for you too.

STARGAZEY PIE

Serves 4–6 (depending on the size of the fish)

6 pilchards or small mackerel, herring or sardine. Fillet the fish but retain the heads on, or ask the fishmonger to do it
150 g prawns
150 g skinless firm white fish, like cod
3 eggs, hard boiled, shelled and chopped
1 medium onion, finely chopped
50 ml white wine
250 ml double cream
Juice of ½ lemon
25 g butter
Couple of stems of parsley, chopped
1 tbsp plain flour
250 ml fish stock (use a ¼ of a cube dissolved in hot water)
250 g puff pastry

Heat up a pan and gently cook the onion in butter. Slowly add the wine, lemon juice, cream, fish stock and flour, stirring. Add the cod to the sauce and cook gently for 2–3 minutes, flaking the fish. Hard-boil the eggs, peel and slice. Cut the filleted pilchards in half and place them in a shallow oven-proof dish and add the sauce, cod, prawns and eggs. Season with salt and pepper. Roll out the pastry and cover the mixture. Carefully make 6 slits in the pastry and insert the pilchard heads staring up 'stargazey'. Place in a preheated oven 200°c/gas 6 for 30–40 minutes.

Serve with boiled potatoes and green vegetables such as green beans.

The book *The Mousehole Cat* by Antonia Barber and Nicola Bayley was something of a hit with my daughters and a visit to Mousehole cemented this as a must-have dish. I've always been puzzled by the inclusion of bacon in the recipe, as the tradition was that the catch saved the villagers from starvation and that was why all the fish, traditionally seven varieties, were baked into the pie. How come there was spare bacon around if they were starving? Add bacon if you want but I never did.

RICK'S AKEE AND SALTFISH

Serves 3–4

450 g salt cod, soaked in water 8 hours/overnight
(change the water at least once)
1 tin ackee, drained
1 onion, finely chopped
1 red pepper chopped seeds removed
1 green pepper chopped and de-seeded
1 scotch bonnet or Caribbean red pepper, chopped and
de-seeded (note this is a hot variety, take care)
2 tbsp sunflower oil
½ cup coconut cream
1 tbsp fresh thyme

Heat the oil in a large frying pan. Add the onion and peppers and fry until softened over a medium heat, about 5 minutes. Add the Chilli and stir. Drain the salt cod. Make sure bones are removed. Rinse in fresh water. Pat the cod dry and add to the pan with the ackee and fry for 5–6 minutes breaking up the cod with a wooden spoon as you go along.

Add the thyme, coconut cream and a taste of pepper and stir in. Serve with roasted green bananas and yams.

When I was on the council, my fellow councillor for the Cowley Road area that I represented was Valerie Ricketts. We worked together very well and became good friends. Her restaurant 'Ricks', was a place to hang out and chat with her about council business while her sons got on with the business of serving the other customers. This is her recipe, a popular dish in the restaurant, one which I have had many times.

BEST FOR AFRO-CARIBBEAN:
AL AMIN
EASTERN AND
CONTINENTAL STORES
MAROC DELI

PHEASANT CASSEROLE

Serves 6

A brace, i.e. 2, pheasants (get your butcher to pluck and gut
unless you like doing this yourself) • 8 rashers of streaky bacon
1 onion, finely sliced • 400 g mixed wild mushrooms. (Some dried
porcini are also very good in this) • 6 tbsp olive oil
2 tbsp tomato puree • ½ bottle red wine • 100 ml chicken stock
10 juniper berries, crushed • 4 thyme sprigs • 3 cloves

Pre-heat the oven to 200°c/gas mark 6. Heat 2 tablespoons of olive oil
in a casserole dish big enough to take both pheasants snugly. Then
brown the pheasant on all sides. Put the birds into the casserole,
drape with the bacon, and put the whole thing into the oven
uncovered, and roast for 10–15 minutes. Remove from the oven and
leave to cool.

Meanwhile, chop the onion, and halve the mushrooms and cook in
the olive oil. Stir from time to time and gradually turn the heat down
so that they start to sweat rather than fry. Add the cloves, juniper
berries, tomato paste and red wine. Meantime put the bacon from
the pheasant into a large bowl. Cut the legs off the pheasant, slice
down the side of the breastbone to remove the breast meat in 2 neat
portions (keep the wings attached) and put all these into the bowl,
too. Drain any juices from your chopping board into the bowl.

Chop the pheasant carcasses into quarters with a cleaver and return
to the casserole. Then add the stock, a dash more wine and the
pheasant meat and bacon. Season to taste. Cover the casserole and
braise for an hour in the pre-heated oven. Serve with jacket potatoes
or mash. Cabbage of various sorts goes very well.

Pheasants are part of my
childhood. Living in the
countryside close to the
Blenheim Estate, local
poachers would pitch up
with a brace for my parents
fairly regularly. Later as a
student I was employed in
the kitchens of the Bear Hotel
in Woodstock, basically as a
'pheasant plucker'. This was at
the time when Richard Burton
and Elizabeth Taylor were
regular diners. Nowadays I
seem to pick up a 'road kill'
pheasant left by other drivers
on almost every trip to the
Chilterns or Cotswolds. The
best time to eat pheasant is
the four months October–
January.

NOT DEER PARK VENISON CASSEROLE

Serves 4–6

1.5 kg diced venison
1 large onion, finely sliced
1 large carrot, finely diced
1–2 sticks celery, finely diced
50 g butter
2 cloves garlic, crushed
½–1 bottle red wine
Salt and peppe

Mix together and marinade for 2–3 hours (not the butter). Strain and retain the juice. Melt butter in a large heavy pan, add the meat and vegetables and cook gently to soften the vegetables and seal the meat. Pack into a casserole and pour in the marinade. Place in oven at 200°c/gas mark 6 for 1½–2 hours.

Finish with a knob of butter and freshly ground pepper. Serve with baked or mashed potato and seasonal vegetables, and if you like a sauce with it, try crab apple jelly.

You can buy venison from the butcher in the autumn and winter. Alternatively, Magdalen College deer park is full of them and occasionally they do a cull. Enquire at the Porters lodge. Allegedly during the Second World War the college authorities reclassified the deer as vegetables, to avoid having them confiscated by the Ministry of Food. Tempted as many an allotment-holder might be on finding one eating their crops, I don't recommend trying to cull them yourself.

BEST FOR MEAT:
ALDERS
FARMERS' MARKET

SLOW-COOKED ROCK STAR CHICKEN

Serves 4

One 1½ kg free range chicken, plucked and gutted
2 celery sticks, chopped • 1 small onion, peeled and thickly sliced
1 small leek, chopped • 1 carrot, chopped into sticks
2 cloves garlic • 1 bottle red wine • 3 sprigs fresh thyme
2 bay leaves • Sm quantity of fresh sage
50 ml sunflower oil • 1 tbsp cornflour

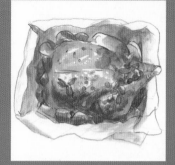

Use a cast-iron casserole dish with lid for this recipe. To marinade the chicken. Cut the chicken into pieces; wings, legs, breast, to maximise meat available (some butchers will do this for you). Pour the wine into a pan and bring to the boil for a couple of minutes. Take it off the heat. Mix the chicken pieces, vegetables, garlic and herbs and pour over the warmed wine. Cover the bowl and leave in the fridge for about 12 hours. Pre-heat the oven to 140°c/gas mark 1. Drain the chicken pieces, veg and herbs in a colander over a bowl. Pick out the chicken pieces and sear them in the oil over a strong heat in the cast iron saucepan for about 3–4 minutes on each side. Remove and keep warm. Then sweat the vegetables (not garlic) in the same pan for about 5 minutes.

Spoon out the fat and return the chicken to the pan. Add the marinade wine, herbs and garlic and a little water if necessary to cover. Bring to the boil, and cover with the lid. Cook in the oven for 60 minutes+ at this low heat. Finally skim off the fat released by the chicken. Dilute the cornflour with 2 tablespoons of water and mix into the chicken juice. Bring to the boil to bind the juices.

Serve with fluffy rice or roast potatoes and some sautéed seasonal mushrooms, along with broccoli or spinach. Try crab apple jelly if you like red-currant sauce with it. Toast the productive life of the chicken with a glass of wine.

I got a funny look from my partner when I mentioned that I was doing this recipe. We had been to see the movie *Take That Waltz* fairly recently and I think she was worried I was about to turn into the male chicken-cooking-obsessed character. She has nothing to worry about. This is the only chicken recipe. I developed it with the help of my neighbour Robert when two of my much loved hens, Beyonce and Shakira finally had to retire. I killed them myself of course and the only way to cook and enjoy 10+ year old chicken is sloooowly.

DESSERTS

In the spirit of simplicity I have
kept the desserts overwhelmingly fruit-based.
'Pudding clubs' abound these days and this
section might rather disappoint them – with
the exception of the generally sweeter historic
recipes. Not much chocolate here. But fresh,
roasted and bottled fruit is so divine that it
seems a missed opportunity not to celebrate
it when it is so readily available.

SEE ALSO:

TROPICAL FRUIT SALAD COWLEY ROAD-STYLE

Serves 4–8 depending on how big the fruit are

1 papaya
1 toad-skin melon
4 mangoes
1 lime, juiced
200 ml coconut milk (from tin)
30 g demerara sugar
50ml dark rum
150 ml crème fraiche
Sprig of mint

Make sure you buy ripe fruit. De-seed, peel, and remove the pips as necessary. Cut into a mixture of chunks and slices. Mix together in a large bowl. Mix the lime juice, rum and demerara sugar together dissolving the sugar. Pour over the fruit and allow to marinade for 10 minutes. Stir fruit again.

Scatter a little more sugar on top to taste and add the mint leaves for decoration. Serve with coconut milk or crème fraiche.

There are plenty of less common fruit varieties to be picked up in the green grocers shops. This is something that mixes some of the exotic best to be found on Cowley Road.

BEST FOR EXOTIC FRUIT:
SIMPLI FRESH
NOOR

CHERRY CLAFOUTIS

Serves 6–8

500 g morello cherries (the sharp ones)
Use whole unless you don't like spitting out the stones
400 ml whole milk
200 g plain flour
120 g caster sugar
3 free range eggs
80 g butter, melted
Pinch salt

Pre-heat the oven to 200°c/gas mark 6. Grease a 30-cm tart dish with butter. De-stalk the cherries and remove bad or damaged ones. Mix the flour, sugar and salt in a large bowl. Beat the eggs and add. When the batter is smooth mix in the melted butter. Then gradually add the milk, mixing well.

Put the cherries into the dish and gently pour the batter over them. Bake for 30 minutes until golden and firm. Allow to cool before serving with crème fraiche or plain yoghurt.

My next door neighbours have a magnificent cherry tree. So magnificent, that about half of it leans over into my garden. The birds really rate it too, so picking cherries can be something of a battle of wills, though local cats finally earn their keep in my eyes at this point in the year, about mid-June. If the birds get them there are always some cherries in the shops.

BEST FOR DESSERTS:
MILLEFEUILLE
GERMAN BAKERY VAN
GREEN VILLAGE

ROAST QUINCE

Serves 4

2–3 quinces, preferably large
1 orange, juiced and the skin shaved
1 lemon, juiced
200 ml red wine
200 g caster sugar
4 tbsp maple syrup or runny honey
4 cloves
1 vanilla pod split and seeds, scraped
1 star anise
400 ml water

Pre-heat the oven to 140°c/gas mark 1. Put the sugar, water, wine and lemon juice in a pan and bring to the boil. Cut the quinces in half, core and peel them. Keep the skin and cores. Place the halved quinces in the pan and add the cores and skins. Simmer for 25–30 minutes.

Remove the halved quinces and place them in a shallow baking dish. Add the spices, orange strips and juice, about 150 ml of the cooking liquid and the maple syrup. Place in the oven and bake for 30 minutes. Serve with ice cream or cream. This recipe has the potential to be a Christmas dessert

The cooked pieces, if there are any left, are very versatile. They can be eaten with rice pudding or in a salad. Or they can accompany pork or strong meat like game. So it is worth cooking more than you really need if you can lay your hands on them. They are best kept in the fridge in the spare cooking juice for several days. The cooking juice itself can be poured over ice cream. The Spanish make *membrillo* a kind of jelly, from quinces, which they eat with cheese, but that is another story.

Quinces are a fruit that most people don't cultivate. It is understandable if space is limited, because unlike other orchard fruits they can only be eaten cooked. Even when ripe they are rock hard and are difficult to cut. Nonetheless they are popular as a kind of collective endeavour on some allotments sites and in community gardens and are readily available in shops. They are very distinctive for their furry skins and unusual almost rose-like aroma. They can be cooked with other fruit, like apples and can add an unusual fragrance to an apple pie, but you will need to either part-cook them first or chop the quince into really small pieces. I prefer to cook them on their own.

FIRST OF THE SPRING RHUBARB

Serves 4

500 g rhubarb
1 orange
2 vanilla pods
2 tbsp Demerara sugar or crab apple jelly (see p xx)
150 g crème fraiche

Pre-heat the oven to 150°c/gas mark 2. Cut the rhubarb into 5cm lengths. Lay it out in a baking dish. Grate the zest of half the orange on top. Add the vanilla pods, splitting them open and scattering some of the seeds. Add the pods, the sugar and the juice from the orange. Bake in the oven for 15 minutes. Be careful not to leave it too long or it will dry out. Serve with crème fraiche or on its own.

If you want to make a more substantial but less pretty version when the rhubarb has grown larger, try rhubarb crumble.

Rhubarb is such a strange fruit. Actually it isn't a fruit, but we treat it as one. It appears in the shops from mid-January and can be picked on allotments from about mid-March especially if 'forced'. This recipe works best with the early pink shoots. Eating the first rhubarb always feels like the celebration of the arrival of spring. This has to be one of the easiest desserts to make.

SUMMER PUDDING

Serves 6

250 g Raspberries or loganberries
250 g Strawberries
250 g Blackcurrants or redcurrants
250 g Gooseberries
Most of a loaf of white bread
200 g white sugar (more if you have a lot of gooseberries)

If you like your summer pudding Italian-style add a bottle of Valpolicella to the sugar and dissolve before adding to the fruit.

Top and tail the fruit as appropriate. Cut the strawberries in half if they are large. Getting the fruit off the stalks of redcurrants and blackcurrants can be fiddly. It doesn't matter if some end up in the mix. Pulling them out as you eat can be fun. My daughters used to refer to them as 'fruit bones'. Place the fruit in a large pan with about 500 ml water and cook gently for 15–20 minutes. Add the sugar about half way through and make sure it is fully dissolved. The fruit should be reduced but with plenty of liquid.

Remove the crusts from the bread (slice it up if not already sliced). Discard the crusts. Place a layer of bread in a dish to line it. Ladle in some of the fruit mix. Add another layer of bread on top of the fruit. Ladle in more fruit. Add another layer of bread. Repeat until the dish is full. Top off with the last of the fruit and juice, making sure to cover all the bread. Place in the fridge with something heavy on top of the final mix (a bowl of water perhaps) and leave for at least 6 hours. This allows the juice to soak fully into the bread and the whole mix to meld together. Remove from fridge and serve with yoghurt or cream.

Summer pudding is one of those desserts where whatever summer fruits are in the shops or on the allotment can be put to use and produce a wonderful result. The secret is to make sure there is enough liquid and it is best to keep it in the fridge for 24 hours before eating. In reality the proportions of fruit don't matter that much as long as there is a reasonable variety.

Cooking apples can be huge and their skins are so distinctively greasy. In the autumn they are readily available from shops and often free from allotment holders or people with a tree in their garden. It is a shame to let them go to waste.

BEST FOR COOKING APPLES:
FARMERS' MARKET

BAKED APPLES

Allow one cooking apple per person, so this serves 6

6 Bramley cooking apples
100 g raisins, currants or with mixed peel
50 g brown sugar
50 g butter

Core the apples. Score the skin right around the circumference to stop the apple bursting when being cooked. Fill the cored hole with a fruit/peel mix to taste and add brown sugar. Seal top and bottom with butter. Sprinkle with a little extra sugar to taste.

Place in a baking dish with a small amount of water and put in an oven at 200°c/gas mark 6. Cook for 20 minutes, or a little longer if the apples are large.

Serve with custard, cream or ice cream.

LOW-HANGING RASPBERRIES WITH RICOTTA

Serves 4

500 g raspberries or loganberries
250 g ricotta
1 lemon
3 tbsp caster sugar

Grate the lemon and mix with the sugar. Place the raspberries on a large plate. Slice the ricotta finely and place the pieces over the raspberries. Sprinkle with the lemon sugar.

I remember as a child our dog finding the raspberry canes in the garden one summer. Every morning she would innocently wander out of the house and return a little while later having snaffled all the low hanging fruit (now I know where that phrase comes from!). They and loganberries trained along a garden wall have the same effect on small children when they discover them, so why not indulge them and yourself?

BEST FOR RICOTTA:
IL PRINCIPE

PRESERVES

Preserves originate from the days before fridges. Fruit and vegetables spoiled before refrigeration unless preserved and the autumn was the time for all kinds of pickling, jam making and the like. Just because most people have fridges these days is no reason for not making jams, chutneys or more recent additions to the store cupboard like pesto. Preserves are about seasonal abundance and not wasting it and they are both a celebration of that abundance – stretching it into winter and beyond – and being frugal and thrifty. Not bad values to have and share. With a little experimentation these recipes can be applied to many other fruits for jam making, or vegetable/ fruit mixtures or chutneys. The principles once mastered can then be fairly readily applied to bottling fruit or making pickles. These recipes are just a taster of the possibilities.

SEE ALSO:

PICKLED WALNUTS p22

OXFORD MARMALADE p27

HORSERADISH SAUCE p29

BRITISH BASIL PESTO

This is enough for a couple of meals for four. If you have the basil and want to make it in the quantities that I do, just increase the ingredients proportionally.

200 g fresh basil (after stalk removal)
200 g pine nuts or walnut/pine nut mix
100 g parmesan or pecorino cheese
3 cloves garlic
6 tbsp olive oil
1 tbsp melted butter
Small quantity of salt

Remove the stalks and damaged leaves. You can keep a certain amount of the soft fleshy stalk and flower heads. Combine the ingredients together in a food mixer and blend until they are a smooth paste. Best to pour the olive oil in gradually through the top as you go along.

Serve direct with a pasta dish, tossed with new potatoes, or as part of a pizza topping and season with freshly ground black pepper, or pack tightly into clean jars and cover the top with a little olive oil to seal, before storing in the fridge.

I absolutely love making pesto. But 25 five years ago it wasn't really feasible to grow basil outdoors regularly in England. Global warming has changed all that, and in 2014 I got not one but two crops of basil grown outdoors, for the first time. As pesto is one of my all-time favourite sauces I grow a lot of basil on my allotment and making pesto is one of the most reliable of household rituals. I generally make enough to last for at least 6 months in jars in the fridge.

BEST FOR FRESH HERBS:
EASTERN AND
CONTINENTAL STORES
SIMPLI FRESH
MAROC DELI

Chutney is a great way of preserving crop gluts and using then later on. Of course freezers help quite a bit these days, but chutney brings an added dimension to quite a few foods, notably with cheese, charcuterie meats/meze, all kinds of Indian foods or even with baked potatoes. There are loads of different kinds of possible chutneys using excess produce, or just things you like in chutney – apple, green tomato, plum, courgette, pear and pumpkin are all suitable. Normally they are made at the end of the season before the frost gets things or the fruit is about to spoil. The basic principles are the same whatever variety you make. Allow half a day to do this. The chopping can be time consuming. Don't use a food-processor, the results are always disappointingly sloppy. This is a courgette and green tomato chutney. You can vary quantities according to availability – but keep the proportions.

BEST FOR HERBS AND SPICES:
TAHMID STORES
NOOR
MAROC DELI

END OF SEASON COURGETTE AND GREEN TOMATO CHUTNEY

1 kg green tomatoes (they can be ripe too)
1 kg courgettes, chopped fairly small (usually the overlarge ones at the end of the season)
500 g cooking apples peeled, cored and sliced
2 medium onions finely chopped
500 g dates, chopped in half • 250 g raisins
500 g demerara sugar • 700 ml cider vinegar
30 g mustard powder • 10 g turmeric
1 fresh chilli, deseeded and chopped
Pinch of salt

Spice bag – This should be a piece of muslin with the following tied up inside:
50–70 g fresh root ginger, roughly peeled and bruised
10 cloves
2 tsp black peppercorns

Put the whole lot into a large preserving pan and bring slowly to the boil, stirring. Allow to simmer for at least 1½ hours. Keep an eye on it to ensure it doesn't burn on the bottom of the pan. Possibly add a little more vinegar if it looks as if it might. It should be well reduced, thick and glossy, but with the chunks of veg still recognisable, i.e. not sloppy/watery. When it has reached this consistency, remove the spice bag and discard the contents and pour the chutney into warm sterilised jars. Make sure the jars have vinegar-proof lids or line them with grease-proof paper or they will rust quite quickly! Chutney is best left to mature somewhere cool and dark for a couple of months.

FORAGED PLUM JAM

2 kg plums
1 kg granulated white sugar/jam making sugar
½ lemon
A little water

Wash the fruit and pick out any that are going bad. If the fruit is firm enough take a serrated knife and stone the fruit. Put in a large stainless steel pan with about 100 ml water and cook over a low heat until soft. Stir in the sugar and add the lemon juice. If the stones have been removed the sugar should be 'jam-making sugar' i.e. with added pectin, or it won't set. Turn up the heat to ensure it boils vigorously. Stir to ensure the mixture doesn't stick to the bottom of the pan and burn.

The jam should begin to set after about 20–30 minutes. You can test for this by taking out a small amount and putting it on a plate to cool. If it is setting it will go crinkly when you push your finger through it. If it doesn't it needs to cook more.

Meanwhile prepare your jars. Make sure they are clean and dry and place them on trays in the oven at a low heat. This will warm them enough to withstand the hot jam. When the jam is ready, take it off the heat, set out the warmed jars and ladle the jam in. Put the tops on immediately and allow to cool. This will seal the jars as the cooling jam contracts.

I am particularly fond of plum jam because my neighbours have a huge plum tree in their front garden. Probably an Early Laxton, it fruits before the end of July producing small round golden red plums in abundance. They fall all over the pavement and street and call out to be gathered up, which I do, producing the first jam of the season. Urban foraging at its best. Plums are not the easiest fruit to make into jam because they don't set that easily and you have to remove the stones or fish them out as you go along. But the result is well worth the effort. This recipe is low sugar by commercial jam standards, but allows the plum flavour to come to the fore. If you find this too tart, add more sugar.

I have an aged crab apple tree in my garden. It was probably planted for the glorious pink blossom in mid-April, but in a good year it also produces an abundance of tiny crab apples. They are completely inedible except when made into jelly. But the jelly is beautiful as well as tasty.

TRANSLUCENT CRAB APPLE JELLY

It is wonderful on toast for breakfast, but it also complements other things like venison.

2 kg crab apples
1 kg granulated sugar
1 lemon
A handful of fresh mint
2 litres water

Wash and sort the crab apples. Halve the larger ones. It is okay to leave in those with some bruising and discolouration. Place them in a large stainless steel pan with the water and the mint. Bring to the boil and cook until they are a mush. Take a large mixing bowl and strain the whole mixture through a muslin cloth. The juice will be a reddish pink. Hang the apple mush somewhere safe and allow it to drip into the bowl for at least a couple of hours.

Discard the apple/mint mush. Return the juice to the pan and warm. Add the sugar and the juice of the lemon and bring to the boil. Cook until the juice has reduced by at least a third. It will then begin to thicken. It is ready when it begins to thicken and starts to look gloopy. Stir every so often to avoid any sticking to the pan and burning. The caramelised flavour will affect the whole batch. Remove a spoonful to a plate and check to see if it has begun to set by allowing it to cool. If it crinkles when you push your finger through it, it has. Be careful to ensure that it really has set because there is nothing worse than 'jelly' that isn't jelly!

When you are confident it will set, pour it into jars, seal and allow to cool. Admire the translucent pink result.

CONVERSION CHARTS

I have worked to metric measurements in this book with the exception of historic recipes where conversion somehow seemed inappropriate. Not everybody uses metric, and some measurements are by spoonful in any case, so these conversion tables are for use as required.

Convention dictates that when converting from ounces to grams that 1 ounce = 25 grams though the exact weight equivalent is 28 g, which is hard to do the multiples of.

WEIGHT

Ounces (oz)		Grams (g)
1	•	25
2	•	50
3	•	75
4	•	100
5	•	125
6	•	150
7	•	175
8	•	200
9	•	225
10	•	250
11	•	275
12	•	300
13	•	325
14	•	350
15	•	375
1lb	•	400

VOLUME

Imperial	ml	spoons
	5	1 teaspoon (tsp)
	10	1 dessertspoon
½ fluid ounce	15	1 tablespoon (tbsp)
1 fl oz	30	
2 fl oz	60	
5 fl oz (1/4 pint)	150	
10 fl oz (1/2 pint)	300	
15 fl oz(3/4pint)	450	
20 fl oz(1 pint)	600	
1¼ pint	750	
1¾ pint	1 litre	

OVEN TEMPERATURES

Gas mark	Celsius (c)	Fahrenheit (f)
1	140	284
2	150	302
3	160	320
4	180	374
5	190	392
6	200	410
7	210	428
8	220	446
9	240	464

The oven temperatures are for fan assisted ovens. For fanless ovens the general rule is to increase the given temperature by 20°c.

CHAPTER SIX

Growing and shopping

One of the principles I have applied to the recipes in this book is that, apart from the fact that they have some particular story attached either personal or Cowley Road-related, they are all made from ingredients available from the shops on or around Cowley Road or from other local sources such as the farmers' market, the 'veg van', allotment or garden produce, or by local foraging.

LOCAL KNOWLEDGE

While these things are inevitably about personal taste and shops do have a habit of changing over time, indeed with remarkable rapidity on Cowley Road, I have put all this nosing around to use and nominated some of the best places to find a selection of the ingredients used. Feel free to use it as a locally-researched reference point for your own exploration.

Finding ingredients in shops is fun, but you cannot beat the freshness and pleasures of growing your own. This is why I have included a basic 'grow it yourself' guide which is drawn from over 35 years of my own accumulated experience of what will, and will not, grow in kitchen gardens and on allotments in the area. I have rented plots on three different sites as I have moved around during that time and combined that experience with the wisdom of several fellow allotmenteers. For those not familiar with allotments, it might surprise some to know just how wide the range of produce grown on them can be, reflecting of course the variety of cultural heritages that allotment gardeners in east Oxford bring to their plots. Foraging has its place even in an environment as urban as east Oxford and I have included a simple guide to some of the more fruitful opportunities.

GROWING YOUR OWN

There is a well-established tradition of stepping outside the constraints of the cash economy through home cultivation. The kitchen garden, the allotment, small-scale market gardening and even the window box have all played a role in providing a supplement to the wages paid to working class families so adding to the variety they could bring to the table. Since enclosure in the mid 19th century, allotments have played a significant role in providing fresh fruit and vegetables and the tradition is very much alive and well with 36 allotment sites in Oxford, 14 of them in east Oxford. Nowadays rents at about £30 per annum per plot are only about one sixth in real terms of what a labourer would expect to have paid 100 years ago.

Just as it has been for over 100 years, growing your own can provide a significant supplement to a household diet, and soil and climate in east Oxford are very favourable. Allotments are popular, and many have waiting lists. The shift towards letting space out in half, quarter or even micro plots has attracted people who have not seen themselves as growers before, and they allow for a more informal engagement.

There are a number of restaurants on Cowley Road that include locally grown food in their menus; more than might be imagined. La Capannina had two allotments on the East Ward site where they grew spinach, courgettes and garlic as well as herbs such as parsley and basil, which was supplemented by a kitchen garden at the back of the restaurant providing figs, pears, cherries and tomatoes for the table. The BBC 'Food Programme' featured their commitment to local growing in a programme in the 1990s. The Jamaican Hi-Lo grow cabbages, beans including kidney beans and runner beans, along with peppers, chillies and tomatoes for the kitchen on their allotment.

In the last decade community gardens have sprung up in east Oxford. The most ambitious and well-established is the Barracks Lane Community Garden, a tiny experimental haven of growing and community empowerment on a former council garage site. Bee-keeping, bread making, permaculture and composting courses mix with seasonal festivals and celebrations on a site filled with flowers, herbs and fruit trees, while events showcasing local bands spread the word on Cowley Road.

Many allotment sites these days are mainly if not entirely, organic. It didn't used to be that way, with a widespread culture of using herbicides, pesticides and artificial fertilisers. As recently as 1993 the *Oxford Mail* could run a news story about an allotment open day with an admittedly punning headline 'Openly organic' – the horticultural practice that dare not speak its name!

Barracks Lane Community Garden proudly presents:

FORMIDABLE VEGETABLE
SOUND SYSTEM

**with a side serving of sweet reggae tunes &
world beats from DJ Baps & Nico D + raffle**

Sat 6th July 2013   7pm - 10pm
the Bully, Cowley Road, Oxford

**Grow Food Everywhere
World Solo Tour 2013**
£8 / £6.50. A fundraiser for
Barracks Lane Community
Garden and a warm-up for
Cowley Road Carnival 2013
wegottickets.com/event/226654
Questions: barrackslanefundraiser@yahoo.co.uk

*Formidable Vegetable Sound System
is an uplifting new global experiment
in 'ecological eduatainment'. Mashing
together speakeasy electroswing-style
wonk and live ukulele quirk with a side
serving of Radish Beets, this Australian
festival sensation turns sustainability
into an epic dancefloor experience.*

For more on this great band: www.formidablevegetable.com
Discover the wonderful BLCG: www.barrackslanegarden.org.uk

Allotments are ideal for households with no garden, small gardens, or gardens for which other purposes are a priority, such as space for children to play. Starting to grow your own can seem daunting and it isn't as easy as so many TV gardening programmes make out. Hard work and failure both go with the territory, but so do wonderful surprises, great fellowship and enormous satisfaction. There are plenty of good books on starting out growing fruit, veg and herbs, but these are recommendations drawn from over 35 years of growing in east Oxford soils.

BEST VEGETABLES TO GROW YOUR OWN

If you manage to grow all these you will be the envy of your allotment neighbours and will hardly need to go to a shop for vegetables all year. It is a good idea to decide whether you are growing vegetables that are difficult to find in the shops, are expensive to buy, are growing them for their attractiveness in the garden or on the plot, or simply because they are easy to grow. I always recommend new allotmenteers to grow potatoes in their first season because there is a tangible sense of achievement with the first crop, even though they aren't very expensive to buy. Here are my top 'picks'.

Potatoes, especially early varieties (Arran Pilot, Maris Peer), classics, (Desiree) salad crop varieties (Charlotte) and unusual/hard to buy such as like Pink Fir Apple, which are also resistant to blight and good for storage.
Spinach and chard, rainbow chard looks lovely in a garden.
Beans, runner beans, broad beans and French beans are all worth growing.
Squash, keep well and taste delicious. Plant sweetcorn amongst the beans and squash and you have the 'three sisters', Mayan-style.
Courgettes, easy to grow, very productive.
Tomatoes, markedly better flavour than shop-bought. Easy to grow. Best in a poly tunnel or greenhouse. Gardener's delight which have small fruit which ripen quickly and can be frozen whole are good to start out with.
Leeks, available when hardly anything else is.
Onions, the essential cook's companion and always look impressive on the plot.
Purple sprouting broccoli, sensational flavour and long cropping.
Peas, children love them straight from the pod, mangetout or 'green sweeties' as my children called them.
Salad crops, lettuce, rocket and a huge range of other salad crops such as lamb's lettuce. Don't forget radishes and cucumbers too.
Beetroot, my favourite root vegetable and stores well, raw or pickled.

Cabbage, versatile, available summer and winter.
Parsnips, great winter standby and lovely roasted.
Carrots, delicious raw as well as cooked.
Kale, the 'super food' of the 21st century.
If you have the space and the ground is well drained,
Asparagus can be very rewarding after a couple of years.

BEST HERBS TO GROW YOUR OWN

Most herbs are pretty hardy and can be grown in gardens or window boxes. Having them close to the kitchen is a good idea. My favourites are:
Garlic, traditionally planted on the shortest day and harvested on the longest.
Chives another member of the onion family, ideal chopped in salads.
Parsley, a cook's staple. Flat leaf is the more versatile.
Rosemary, a great addition to stews.
Mint, great in salads and makes a cool refreshing drink. Grow in a pot; it can quickly take over a garden bed.
Sage, a traditional staple in stuffings.
Thyme used for tea, medicinal purposes and as a flavouring in roasts and stews.
Bay particularly useful in soups.
Lovage can be an acquired taste, it is quite strong, but a good addition to salads. Some similarity to celery.
Coriander a must in South Asian cookery.
Marjoram good with fish or meat dishes.
Sorrel the red veined slightly bitter leaves are a good addition to salads.
Oregano very good in stews and topping home-made pizza
Fennel leaves can be used fresh or dried. Anise flavoured seeds used in both sweet and savoury dishes.
Basil, the queen of the herbs, wonderful in all Mediterranean dishes, but not so easy to grow from seed.

Some herbs like **nasturtiums** and **borage** are very good for their flowers.

Growing some flowers helps the pollinators, look pretty and give months of cut flowers to take home too. My favourite is **sweet pea** because it smells so wonderful and the more you pick the more you get.

BEST FRUIT TO GROW YOUR OWN

Fruit growing is a more ambitious undertaking because the trees take up a lot of space. Although not strictly a fruit, rhubarb is one of the easiest to grow and is available for cropping long before any 'real' fruit.
Fruit trees, (also known as 'top fruit' as opposed to soft fruit), requires a large garden, some skill with training along walls, cordons, espalier etc, or an indulgent allotment association. But if any of these apply and space permits, the following are well worth growing:
Apples, both cookers and eaters. England's favourite fruit. There are about 4,000 varieties world- wide.
Pears, crop very well but difficult to store.
Plums, can be very prolific and make marvellous pies and jam.
Greengages, very similar to plums but earlier and smaller. An early summer treat .
Cherries, if you can keep the birds off them, are well worth it.
Soft fruit takes up less space and can be hugely productive. Think about what you might do with 5 kg of blackcurrants before you plant. Do you have the freezer space or like jam making? All these do well:
Raspberries, **loganberries**, **gooseberries**, **blackcurrants** and **redcurrants**, **strawberries**, and **cultivated blackberries.**

Keeping the birds off them as they ripen is often the biggest challenge.

IN FAVOUR OF FORAGING

Foraging has a long tradition and I am a committed advocate of the activity. Blackberries and sloes were commonly found in the wild in medieval times and would have supplemented the residents of Bartlemas's diet in the autumn. Robert Plot refers to 'the hedges at Cowley and near to Oxford' being particularly well endowed with elderberry.

Today allotment holders like me look to the hedges that surround their sites for foraging opportunities still. Foraging enables you to relate to seasonality first hand – for instance wild fruit is only ripe in the autumn – and can put you in touch with wider food politics. It is an activity that while empowering and delighting also reminds us of the wider

history of food and about issues of poverty, survival and inequality.

Several of my recipes involve foraged crops and good crops can be found in hedgerows, parks and open spaces at the right time of year. Easy to find, easy to use are:

Blackberries the commonest and most recognisable of forage crops.

Elder, both flowers and berries are good in different ways.

Mushrooms, but be sure you know what you are picking. See my further reading section for advice.

Wild damson/Bullace, very common in hedgerows.

Rosehips or rowan berries, for jelly.

Nettles for soup.

Sloes, sloe gin is a real winter treat.

Wild garlic, for soup. I still recall the free-range hens we kept when I was a child finding wild garlic, with an interesting effect on the flavour of their eggs!

Dandelions, good in salads.

Hazelnuts, if the squirrels don't get there first.

When foraging, be sure to take from public spaces not other people's property, unless you have permission. Flowers and fruit belong to no one, but roots in the soil belong to the landowner – as do planted crops, including fruit in orchards.

DIRECTORY OF COWLEY ROAD FOOD SUPPLIERS

This is a complete guide to the food shops on Cowley Road and immediate surrounds. Some are better than others and many are specialists in something. Taken together they provide a range of supplies to satisfy practically every culinary taste.

Al Amin, 216 Cowley Road. Halal butchers and grocers.

Alder's Butchers, 224 Cowley Road. Butcher and game.

Atif Superstore, 256 Cowley Road. Halal meat and poultry, continental foods, fish.

Baltic Foods, 88 Cowley Road. Eastern European and Russian food.

Best Buy, 76 Magdalen Road. Halal meat fruit and vegetables, Indian sweets.

Co-operative, 217 Cowley Road. Supermarket.

Cultivate veg van, outside Rusty Bicycle, Hurst St. Fresh fruit vegetables and herbs in season. Thursday 4–7pm.

Eastern and Continental Stores, 152 Cowley Road. Halal meat groceries and vegetables.

East Oxford Farmers' Market, East Oxford Primary School, Union Street, OX4 1JP. Wide range of stalls selling fresh local produce; some seasonal only. Saturdays 10am–1pm.

German Bakery of Windsor, van outside SS Mary & John Church, Cowley Road. German baked goods and deli. Fridays 11.15–11.45 am (www.thegermanbakery.co.uk).

Gibbons Bakery, 16 Hertford St. Bakery, eggs, honey, samosas.

Green Village, 78A Cowley Road. Lebanese groceries, French patisseries, Arabic sweets, fresh halal meats, eastern spices.

Jing Jing Oriental Foods, 188 Cowley Road. Chinese Japanese, Korean and Vietnamese foods.

Il Principe, 82 Cowley Road. Italian deli.

Maroc Deli, 66 Cowley Road. Halal meat, groceries, fruit and veg.

Meli, 51A Cowley Road. Greek deli and wholefoods.

Millefeuille, 86 Cowley Road. Patisserie, Algerian and oriental sweets.

Morrisons Local, 381-383 Cowley Road. Supermarket.

Noor Halal, 106-107 Magdalen Road, OX4 1RG. Fruit and vegetables, halal meat.

Polski Sklep Zubr, 124 Cowley Road. Polish deli.

Sainsbury's, 140-142 Cowley Road. Supermarket.

Simpli Fresh, 236-238 Cowley Road. Fresh fruit and vegetables incl. home delivery.

Sobieski Mini Market, 132 Cowley Road. Polish supermarket and deli.

Tahmid Stores, 53 Cowley Road. Asian Supermarket including fish, halal meat, herbs and spices. Also wholesale.

Tesco Metro, 153-167 Cowley Road. Supermarket.

Uhuru, 48 Cowley Road. Wholefoods and organic deli.

Wild Honey, 111 Magdalen Road. Organic deli and health food store.

RECIPE INDEX

FURTHER READING

There are a number of books that I have referred to in putting my own together. These are the most important sources.

Alden's Oxford Guide (Bocardo Press, 1908).

Attlee, James: *Isolarion: A Different Oxford Journey* (Black Swan, London, 2009).

Beeton, Isabella (Mrs): *Household Management* (Ward, Lock and Co, 1936).

Bramwell, David: *The Cheeky Guide to Oxford* (Cheekyguides Ltd, 2000).

Carroll, Lewis: *Alice's Adventures in Wonderland* (Heinemann Ltd, 1933).

Clevely, Andi: *The Allotment Seasonal Planner and Cookbook* (Collins, 2008).

Crouch, David and Ward, Colin: *The Allotment: Its Landscape and Culture* (Faber & Faber, 1998).

Dawson E and Royal SR (eds): *An Oxfordshire Market Gardener: The Diary of Joseph Turrill of Garsington 1863–67* (Alan Sutton, 1993).

Dale, Lawrence: *Towards a Plan for Oxford City* (Faber & Faber, 1944).

Davidson, Alan: *The Oxford Companion to Food* (Oxford University Press, 1999).

De la Falaise, Maxime: *Seven Centuries of English Cooking* (Weidenfeld & Nicholson, 1973).

Graham, Malcolm: *Henry Taunt of Oxford; a Victorian Photographer* (The Oxford Illustrated Press, 1973).

Graham, Malcolm and Waters, Laurence: *Cowley and East Oxford Past and Present* (Sutton Publishing, 2002).

Heath, Ambrose: *The Country Life Cookery Book* (Country Life Ltd, 1937).

Hoyles, Martin: *The Story of Gardening* (Journeyman Press, 1991).

Kelly's Street Directories. (1890–1976).

Jakeman, J: *Ralph Ayres' Cookery Book* (Bodleian Library, 2006).

Lalor, Doireann: *Feeding the Gaps: Food Poverty and Food Surplus Redistribution in Oxford* (Oxfordshire County Council, 2014).

Lalor, Doireann and Lefort, Peter: *DinnerTime: A Community Action Handbook* (CAG, 2014).

Lewis-Stempel, John: *Foraging: The Essential Guide to Wild Food* (Right Way, 2012).

Mabey, Richard: *Food for Free* (Fontana, 1975).

Mabey, Richard: *The Full English Cassoulet: Making Do and Other Improvisations in the Kitchen* (Chatto and Windus, 2008).

Panton, Andy: *Fare Stage for Bartlemas: A Personal History of the Cowley Road* (Opta Press, 1986).

Plot, Robert: *The Natural History of Oxfordshire* (Oxford University Press, 1676).

Purves, John: *Notes on the History of Elder Stubbs* (Self-published, 2008).

Radiation Cookery Book (Radiation Ltd, 1938).

Romans, Alan: *The Potato Book* (Frances Lincoln, 2013).

Salmon, Graeme: *Beyond Magdalen Bridge: The Growth of East Oxford* (Oxford Meadow Press, 2010).

Samuel, Raphael: 'Quarry "Roughs": Life and Labour in Headington Quarry 1860–1920. An Essay in Oral History', in Samuel, R (ed): *Village Life and Labour* (RKP, 1975).

Shatford, Suzanne and Williams, Trevor: *The Changing Faces of St Clements and east Oxford (Book 1).* (Robert Boyd, 1997).

Skinner, Annie: *Cowley Road: A History* (Signal Books, 2005).

Spencer, Colin: *The Heretics Feast* (Fourth Estate, 1993).

Sharp, Thomas: *Oxford Replanned* (Architectural Press, 1948).

Surman, Phyl: *Pride of the Morning: An Oxford Childhood* (Alan Sutton, 1992).

Taunt, Henry W: *Oxford Illustrated by Camera and Pen* (Self-published, c 1904).

Taunt, Henry W: *Oxford and its Historical Associations* (Frank Cooper 'privately printed', 1905).

Uglow, Jenny: *A Little History of British Gardening* (Chatto and Windus, 2004).

Uhuru Collective: *Uhuru: A Working Alternative* (Self-published, 1976).

Uhuru Collective: *The Uhuru Cooking Guide* (Self-published, c 1977).

Valter's Oxford and District Directories. 1882–90.

Willes, Margaret: *The Gardens of the British Working Class* (Yale University Press, 2014).

Yurdan, Marilyn: *The Changing Faces of Cowley Road* (Lamplight Publications, 2010).

WEBSITES.

Many of the organisations and businesses referred to have websites. Indeed many primarily operate through them. These websites were accessed and were active during the production of this book.

Abundance Oxford https://abundanceoxford.wordpress.com

Barracks Lane Community Garden
www.barrackslanegarden.org.uk

Cowley Road Carnival www.cowleyroadcarnival.co.uk

Cultivate www.cultivateoxford.org

DinnerTime www.itsdinnertime.org

East Oxford Farmers' Market www.eastoxfordmarket.org.uk

Fairtrade Foundation www.fairtradefoundation.org.uk

Garden Organic www.gardenorganic.org.uk

German Bakery www.thegermanbakery.co.uk

Good Food Oxford www.goodfoodoxford.org

Oxford Botanic Gardens www.botanic-garden.ox.ac.uk

Oxford Hub including Oxgrow Community Garden
www.oxfordhub.org

Oxfordshire History Centre https://oxfordshire.gov.uk/cms/public-site/oxfordshire-history-centre

Restore www.restore.org.uk

School Ethical Supplies Initiative (SESI) www.sesi.org.uk

Vegetarian Society https://www.vegsoc.org

ACKNOWLEDGEMENTS

All the black and white photographs are reproduced by kind permission of Oxfordshire County Council's Oxfordshire History Centre, with the exception of the picture on p38, which is courtesy of Gordon Thompson and the pictures of Uhuru in the 1980s which are by the author.

All colour pictures are by the author except La Capannina, p40 courtesy Gillman and Soame.

I am grateful to Signal Books for permission to reproduce two quotations from Annie Skinner's book *Cowley Road: A History* on p54, to James Attlee and Black Swan for permission to reproduce the quote on p49 from James Attlee's book *Isolarion* and to the History Press for permission to reproduce the extracts from *An Oxfordshire Market Gardener* on pp21-22.

I am grateful to the mapmakers Alex Singleton (www.alexsingleton.biz) and Sebastian Ballard (www.mapman.co.uk) for their illuminating maps, and to Stig (shtiggy.wordpress.com) for permission to reproduce the poster on p120.

*****

Putting this book together has felt like learning to cook; it has involved the co-operation and encouragement of many people in many different ways and I would like to thank them all.

In making sense of the recent history of Cowley Road I have been able to interview people who have played a significant role in its development into the place it is today, including quite a few shopkeepers, restaurant owners and other traders past and present who have given their time to discuss their businesses, the history of Cowley Road from their perspective, and how they come to be where they are now. Often they have spoken for the first time. These include: Valerie Ricketts, Andrew Kuomi, Manju Miah, Roy Gibbons, Andy Alder, Gordon Thompson, Brian Levison, Rupert Griffin, Clinton Pugh, Julian Cottee, Majid Chatar, Rina Melendes, Soran Salih, Carmelina Lawton-Smith (nee Arcucci), Ludmilla Berenis, Agnieszka Gandurka, Reza Khalaj, Jan and Andy Anderson, and my former fellow board members from the Ethnic Minority Business Service including; 'Junior' Lennon, Nawaz Khan and Aziz Rahman.

Other participants on the stage that is Cowley Road include, Mike O'Regan, Mick Ganly, Margaret Gibb, Christine Simm, Sue Gwilliam, Olivier Guillot, Doireann Lalor, Phil Crème, Jacqui Mansfield, Bill Heine, Leonard Pepper, Mary Neave, Chris Church, Andrew Morris, Sr Christine and Sr Margaret Theresa from the Convent of the Incarnation, Sian Charnley, Bert and Stuart Silvester, Greta Smith, Khizer Khan, Jan Bartlett, Hannah Fenton and Elise Benjamin. All provided helpful anecdotes, insights, contacts, or ideas to follow up.

For taking a wider and more reflective perspective, I would like to thank, Hafiz Ladell, Mohammed Alayas, Massoud Ahmed, Annie Skinner, Jamie Attlee and Jon Carpenter for some helpful discussions on the 20th century history of Cowley Road and the surrounding area.

Insights and advice on the local history of east Oxford were provided by Malcolm Graham, Graeme Salmon, Liz Wooley, John Purves, Trevor Williams of the Cowley Local History Society and Helen Drury from the Oxfordshire History Centre, who went to enormous trouble to track down historic photographs and provide them in a useable format.

Fruitful ideas on recipes and growing came from discussions with Eric and Jo Hodges, Mike Kent, Alistair Mallick, Robert Vilain, Samia Shibli, Januz Kempczynski, John Fernandes and Sue Gwilliam.

Help with the process of writing and other creative ideas including illustrations and map making came from conversations with Roman Krznaric, Neil Spencer, Alexandra Harris, Nichola Nixon, Helen Ganly and fellow Writers in Oxford members, Jane Bingham, Denise Cullington and Robert Bullard. Several people read parts of or all of early drafts, and I am particularly grateful to Sue Gwilliam, Hilary Simpson, Robert Vilain, David Robson and Robert Hutchison.

A couple of books came in as important points of departure in terms of inspiration; Jans Ondantje Rolls, *The Bloomsbury Cookbook* (Thames & Hudson 2014) and the Gloucester Road WI, *The Gloucester Road Cookbook*, (Gloucester Road WI 2013). One gave me the idea of writing a book about the culinary delights of a particular street and the other that of mixing up an historical narrative with recipes that illustrate the place and the characters. This book has turned out very different from either, but they helped me clarify what I wanted to do.

I must also thank my daughters Nadine and Alice, for helping me to learn to cook, and for themselves being examples of how to cook. I have learned a huge amount through and from them.

And finally I would like to thank all the customers I have had staying with me through Airbnb over the past 18 months. Virginia Woolf wrote to fellow novelist Katharine Mansfield in 1921 *'I'm in the middle of my novel now, but have to break off, of course to make a little money. I shall write an article on Dorothy Wordsworth and so pay for our new sheets'*. Changing sheets and cooking breakfasts, so earning money from these lovely guests, has funded the writing of this book.

ABOUT THE AUTHOR

Martin Stott has lived in and around Cowley Road for over 35 years. He has been a City councillor, school governor, campaigner and activist. He is Chair of the Divinity Road Area Residents Association (DRARA).

He is author of *'Spilling the beans: a style guide to the new age'* and edited *'City Fields, country gardens: allotment essays'* and has written for a range of media including *the Guardian, New Statesman* and *New Internationalist*. He was a regular contributor to the slow food and environmental magazine *Vole* in the 1970s. He is Deputy Chair of Garden Organic, Chair of the William Morris Society, was a trustee of the Elder Stubbs allotments for 14 years and a founder member of the Ethnic Minorities Business Service. He blogs on growing, gardening, composting and food as Lord Muck. (www.martin-stott.com/)

ABOUT MICHAEL GABRIEL

Painter and illustrator, Michael studied at Massachusetts College of Art, and The Ruskin School of Drawing and Fine Art. He has specialized in animation art direction and background painting, with work on films including *The Snowman, Pink Floyd – The Wall, When The Wind Blows, The Tailor of Gloucester*, and *Pumpkin Moon*.

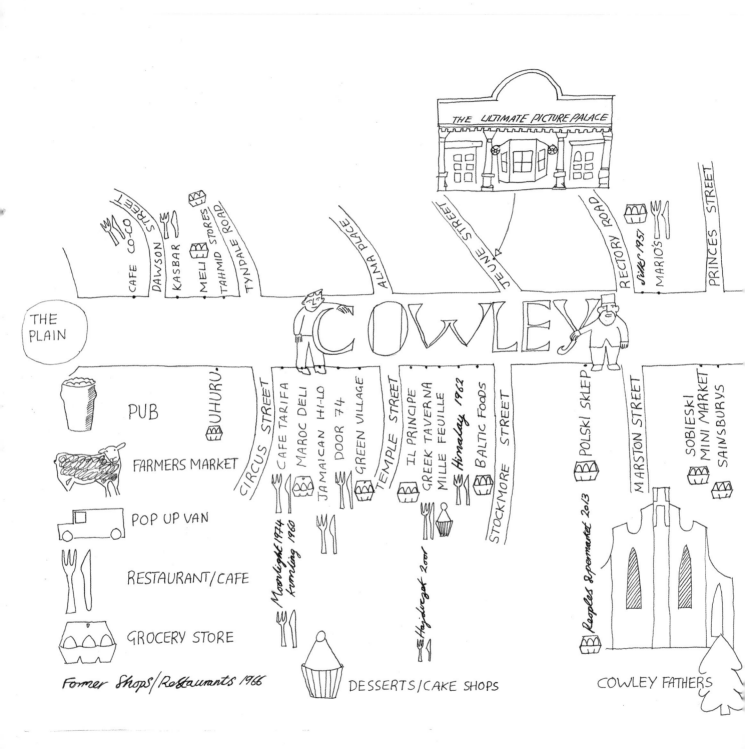

THE ULTIMATE PICTURE PALACE

COWLEY

THE PLAIN

DAWSON STREET

CAFE CO-CO

KASBAR

MELI

TAHMID STORES

TYNDALE ROAD

ALMA PLACE

JEUNE STREET

RECTORY ROAD

Jude's 1957

MARIOS

PRINCES STREET

BUHURU.

CIRCUS STREET

CAFE TARIFA

MAROC DELI

JAMAICAN HI-LO

DOOR 74

GREEN VILLAGE

TEMPLE STREET

IL PRINCIPE

GREEK TAVERNA

MILLE FEUILLE

Himalay 1962

BALTIC FOODS

STOCKMORE STREET

POLSKI SKLEP

Rooples Supermarket 2013

MARSTON STREET

SOBIESKI MINI MARKET

SAINSBURYS

Moonlight 1974

Kumling 1960

Hajducyk 2001

PUB

FARMERS MARKET

POP UP VAN

RESTAURANT/CAFE

GROCERY STORE

Former Shops/Restaurants 1966

DESSERTS/CAKE SHOPS

COWLEY FATHERS